WHO WILL BE IN THE WHITE HOUSE?

PREDICTING PRESIDENTIAL ELECTIONS

RANDALL J. JONES, JR.
UNIVERSITY OF CENTRAL OKLAHOMA

Longman

New York • San Francisco • Boston
London • Toronto • Sydney • Tokyo • Singapore • Madrid
Mexico City • Munich • Paris • Cape Town • Hong Kong • Montreal

Vice President and Publisher: Priscilla McGeehon
Senior Acquisitions Editor: Eric Stano
Senior Marketing Manager: Megan Galvin-Fak
Production Manager: Charles Annis
Project Coordination, Text Design, and Electronic Page Makeup: Pre-Press, Inc.
Cover Design Manager: John Callahan
Cover Designer: Kay Petrunio
Manufacturing Manager: Roy Pickering
Printer and Binder: Courier/Stoughton
Cover Printer: Lehigh Press

Library of Congress Cataloging-in-Publication Data

Jones, Randall J.
    Who will be in the White House? : predicting presidential elections / Randall J.
    Jones, Jr.
       p. cm.
    Includes bibliographical references and index.
    ISBN 0-321-08729-1 (alk. paper)
      1. Presidents—United States—Election—Forecasting. 2. Election forecasting—
United States. I. Title.

JK524 .J65 2001
324.973'001'12—dc21   2001038738

Please visit our website at http://www.ablongman.com

ISBN 0–321–08729–1

CRS—04 03 02 01

10 9 8 7 6 5 4 3 2 1

To Shirley

Contents

Preface

Who will be in the White House? That question is uppermost on nearly everyone's mind every four years as the country goes through the long ritual of choosing a president. Are there ways to know ahead of time with any degree of accuracy who is likely to win the presidency? The answer is "yes," as this book demonstrates. Described in the following pages are recognized forecasting techniques that have been, or could be, applied to predicting the outcome of presidential elections. Typically, the resulting forecasts are grounded in election and voting theory and based on the systematic analysis of observable data.

Chance and Pundits

Of course, some people are attracted to prediction schemes based on mere chance or happenstance. For example, sports-minded prognosticators point to an election pattern among baseball World Series winners that was perfect from 1948 until 1980 (64% of the time through 2000). These link wins by the National League team with Democratic presidential victories; American League wins are paired with Republican victories (reported by Lewis-Beck and Rice 1992, 1-3).

One observer looks at the number of the last digit of presidential election years:

> In the 20th century, there have been eight [now 10, counting Bush in 2000] presidential turnovers, that is, elections when the party holding the Executive Branch lost it to a challenger from the other major party. . . . Three conclusions stand out. First, except for Jimmy Carter's victory in 1976, no presidential turnover has occurred in the middle of a decade—that is, in years ending in "4" or "6". . . . Second, only one turnover occurred at the end of the decade, Republican Richard Nixon's victory over Democrat Hubert Humphrey in 1968. And, third, most turnovers occur in years ending in "0" or "2". (Eckes 1992).

Another writer even considers the possibility of a relationship between presidential elections and phases of the moon (Lord 1996, 112)!

Predictions based on World Series winners, the last digit of election years, or phases of the moon are, of course, interesting and novel, but not a concern of this book. Nor does the book deal with more serious impressionistic prognostications made by informed journalists and other political commentators. No doubt many of the people who sit around tables on television news programs, trading campaign stories and comparing the latest polls from the election horse race, are bright and well informed. But their observations tend to be ad hoc and anecdotal. Moreover, they often appear to succumb to "groupthink" (Janis 1982), in this context a phenomenon in which there emerges a predominant accepted interpretation of the election contest and its presumed outcome, which commentators are reluctant to challenge. Yet it is these commentaries that the public often relies on for clues as to the likely winner of an upcoming election.

Techniques

Rather than reporting chance predictions and pundits' prognostications, this book describes and illustrates systematic election forecasting methods. Some of these techniques are based on the judgment and assessments of experts. More common are techniques that link numerical indicators to election results.

One quantitative approach focuses on the *graphic presentation of individual indicators*. Several chapters include line plots of indicators that identify thresholds or cutpoints, above or below which elections have been won or lost. On page 32 is an example of a forecasting line plot, with win and loss lines marked.

Probably the most common election forecasting technique is *regression*, and applications of it appear frequently in the book. I recognize that many readers may be unfamiliar with this method. Therefore, I will show you what you need to know about regression in order to read this book. My "short course" on this technique appears in the Appendix near the end of the book, beginning on page 143. Also, a glossary of terms used in regression is provided. After reading the explanation in the Appendix, I think you will agree that the basic concept of regression is not complicated and, in fact, is readily understandable. At several points in the book I demonstrate how to produce an election forecast from a single-indicator regression equation. (Turn to page 23 for an example, using a 2000 election forecast.) Notice also that you can calculate your own forecasts for the 2004 election with equations appearing in appendices to some chapters. (An example is on page 38.) Moreover, hypothetical scenarios derived from regression are reported (as in the table on page 121).

Throughout the book I have avoided statistical jargon as much as possible, especially in Chapters 1 through 8. For example, I have tried not to use the term "variance," choosing instead just to say what variance means when I have needed to refer to the concept. In these chapters I have avoided another term, "multivariate," choosing "multi-variable" instead. (In Chapter 9, however, statistical terms appear more frequently, for that is the one chapter that deals with more complex statistical equations or "models.") Also, to enhance the flow of the presentation, I have avoided footnotes. In some cases side comments have been necessary and, of course, I have often needed to cite sources, so these have been placed in parentheses in the text. Usually I have cited the source in which an article, table, or figure first appeared, even though the item may have been published again later.

Chapter Previews

The following description of the chapters' contents provides an overview of the specific forecasting approaches that are covered in the book, many of which apply the techniques just discussed. The first four chapters describe forecasting methods based on surveys of public opinion. Chapter 1 covers *national polls*—"*trial heats*"—in which people are asked their candidate preferences. As you will see, trial heat polls from Labor Day through the fall campaign are often good predictors of the November election's outcome.

In Chapter 2, I identify *bellwether states* (and counties) whose election results have closely mirrored the national vote historically. This means that the outcome of a national election can be forecast by predicting the vote in the bellwether, using state trial heat polls or other methods.

In Chapter 3, we look at a technique based on national surveys in which the public registers its approval or disapproval of the *president's job performance*. Quite often voters' attitudes toward the president are reflected in the extent of their support for the candidate of the president's party. The discussion of public opinion-based forecasting techniques concludes with Chapter 4, which covers election day *exit polls* (which are very short-term forecasts that provide only a few hours of lead time), a novel application of stock market *supply and demand principles* to election forecasting, and a couple of more obscure techniques.

In Chapter 5, the analysis shifts from opinions of the public to the *opinions of experts*. How do well-informed observers view the election environment and the likely outcome? Several techniques that make use of expert assessment of the election contest are described, ranging from Lichtman's well-known application of "13 keys to the White House" to some promising approaches that thus far have been little used for this purpose.

Cyclical patterns have been identified in American elections for more than 100 years by observers who contend that a regular alternation exists in public attitudes and in party affiliation of winning presidential candidates. As is evident in Chapter 6, the approach of some cycle theorists is rather impressionistic, while that of others uses quite sophisticated methods. Evidence from both research styles is reviewed to determine the extent to which such patterns exist.

In Chapter 7, we focus on the process by which presidential candidates are nominated, as well as the ensuing fall campaigns following the conventions, to assess their election forecasting potential. Is the success of a party's nominee in the general election related to his success in early *presidential primaries?* Does it matter whether party *nominating conventions* are smooth-running events or disorderly? And what is the impact of the *fall campaign* on the election outcome?

In Chapter 8, we leave the political arena of the preceding chapters and search in the *national economy* for clues as to likely election outcomes. Is it really "the economy, stupid," as the irrepressible political consultant James Carville tells us? To determine the usefulness of the economy in forecasting elections, I report the strength of linkages between election results and economic growth, interest rates, and several other indicators.

In the last chapter, Chapter 9, as stated in the title, I seek to "put it all together." The focus shifts from individual indicators, often the subject in prior chapters, to *combinations of indicators*. We thus explore the forecasting ability of various groupings of variables proposed by forecasting analysts. Indeed, most of the research undertaken on predicting presidential elections has involved at least two or three indicators. As we will see, usually the forecasts generated by most of these multi-variable equations have been reasonably accurate.

The book's Conclusion is primarily a retrospective on the forecasting experience in the *2000 election*. Various impediments to accurately predicting that unusual election are analyzed.

Acknowledgments

As is typical in books that survey a field of study, few of these ideas are original with me. For the most part, I summarize and explain what others have done and am glad to acknowledge the contribution of these scholars to this book; indeed, there would be no book without their work. Throughout the text I have tried diligently to give credit where credit is due. I also have sought to accurately summarize and fairly evaluate the work of analysts whose techniques and arguments appear in the book, and I hope that I have succeeded in doing so.

I am particularly indebted to the following scholars and their publishers for permitting me to reprint tables or figures from their work, as credited in the text: Alan Abramowitz, Ian Budge, James Campbell, Allan Lichtman, Helmut Norpoth, and Steven Rosenstone.

I very much appreciate the encouragement and help of the talented team at Longman Publishers, especially Eric Stano, senior editor for political science, who facilitated my work, providing on-going support and insightful advice about the manuscript; also publisher Priscilla McGeehon, to whom I first broached the concept for this book when she was visiting our campus; and political science senior marketing manager Megan Galvin-Fak who, also on a campus visit, offered encouragement from her perspective.

I am grateful to colleagues Greg Scott, Steve Garrison, and Tim Baughman for their helpful comments on the manuscript and to Lou Furmanski for providing an agreeable department environment in which to do this work. My thanks also go to several reviewers for their useful feedback and suggestions: Scott Peters, University of Louisville; Harold Stanley, Southern Methodist University; Richard Murray, University of Houston; Thomas J. Baldino, Wilkes University; Amy E. Black, Franklin and Marshall College; and Martin Gruberg, University of Wisconsin. I alone, of course, am responsible for the final product.

Randy Jones

Trial Heat Polls

*People are unpredictable by nature, and
although you can take a nation's pulse, you
can't be sure that the nation hasn't just run
up a flight of stairs, and although you can
take a nation's blood pressure, you can't
be sure that if you came back in twenty
minutes you'd get the same reading.*

E. B. White
The New Yorker
13 November 1948

Undoubtedly, the most obvious way to forecast an election result is to ask voters how they intend to vote. That is, conduct a survey of prospective voters
before an election to ascertain their candidate preferences. Assuming that
they then vote for the candidates they prefer, one should be able to predict
the election outcome on the basis of the survey. (Of course, this all assumes
that E. B. White is wrong and that "the nation hasn't just run up a flight of
stairs"!)

As simple as this approach may appear, in practice it is much less so. If a
national survey of voter preferences among presidential candidates—"trial
heat" poll—is to be useful as an election forecasting tool, it must meet several
requirements. First, the survey must be an accurate reflection of voter preferences at the time it is taken. Survey design—particularly sampling techniques—and implementation must follow sound procedures. Second, the
survey's outcome must be linked to the election outcome. Specifically, a strong
relationship must exist between the public's preferences for the candidates at
the time of the poll and the election result, sufficient to provide an accurate
forecast. Third, the link between the survey and the election outcome must
exist far enough before the election for the poll to be useful as a forecast. The
forecast must lead the election by a sufficiently wide time margin to be of forecasting value.

How well do trial heat polls meet these forecasting requirements?

Survey Methods

We look first at techniques and methods used in survey research. As mentioned, if a pre-election survey of voter preferences for candidates is to effectively forecast those candidates' strength in a subsequent election, it is critical that the survey accurately reflect voter opinion at the time. This is an issue of survey design and execution. The long history of surveys has seen a progressive evolution in the sophistication of methods used, from truly crude efforts to elicit opinion to the reliable techniques used today.

When the first presidential election straw votes were taken in the 1824 campaign, by newspapers in North Carolina and Delaware, survey techniques were haphazard. Opinions were sought from people attending various public gatherings, especially militia group meetings, undoubtedly in no systematic way (Tankard 1992). Later, with the development of statistics as a discipline, the importance of random sampling came to be recognized—but not by everyone conducting surveys.

Inattention to random sampling led to a well-publicized polling failure in the 1936 presidential campaign. This case involved a widely read weekly magazine, the *Literary Digest*. That year the *Literary Digest* mailed questionnaires to about two million people. The magazine had done this in prior elections, and results had been reasonably accurate in 1928 and 1932. But in 1936 a landslide victory was predicted for Landon; Roosevelt, of course, won the landslide. A major problem with the *Literary Digest* poll was that people were chosen from telephone and car owner directories. This biased the sample because it was not random and excluded people who did not have telephones or cars, a large group in 1936. Moreover, many people who received questionnaires did not return them, another source of sample bias. Though a fiasco, this experience did lead to the development of better sampling and interviewing techniques (Field 1983; Squire 1988).

A second well-known problem case occurred at the time of the 1948 presidential election, when major polls failed to predict Truman as the winner over Dewey. Final pre-election surveys picked Dewey by a margin of 5 to 15 percent, when in fact Truman won by 4.4 percent (Clymer 1998). Although pollsters such as Gallup and Roper were using more sophisticated methods than that of the *Literary Digest* in 1936, particularly improvements in identifying probable voters, in this case they stopped polling too soon. Most interviewing for the final Gallup Poll was completed 10 to 12 days before the election. That poll showed that a large share of those surveyed—8.7 percent—still were undecided. Subsequent studies revealed that most undecided people voted for Truman, that a sizable group switched from Dewey to Truman in the last days of the campaign, and that many voters decided to vote only shortly before the election (Gallup 1972, 468–469).

On balance, the polls' incorrect prediction of the 1948 election was due more to pollsters' failure to conduct late pre-election surveys than to problems with survey methods. Nevertheless, the credibility of polling again came under question, with prominent organizations, including the Social Science Research Council, forming study groups to offer advice to pollsters (Buchanan 1986, 222).

Today, techniques for designing and conducting surveys are well refined, at least those used by reputable polling organizations in the United States. We now know that the method of sampling is critical to the accuracy of survey results. The basic rule is that the sample should be randomly selected, so that every voter has as good a chance of being chosen as every other voter does. In practice, sampling is often of randomly selected geographic areas, as in cluster sampling; people in numerous small areas are then interviewed.

In recent years, most national polls have been conducted by telephone, with interviewers calling prospective voters to elicit their opinions. Telephone polling has largely replaced in-person interviewing for several reasons. Face-to-face interviews are more susceptible to bias, such as when the interviewer and interviewee are of different races (Finkel, Guterbock, and Borg 1991). Furthermore, in-person interviews take longer to complete, are more costly, and may subject interviewers to personal danger, especially in rough urban neighborhoods.

The usual approach in telephone surveying is to purchase samples of working phone numbers from firms that specialize in selecting valid samples, such as Survey Sampling, Inc. (**www.ssisamples.com**). Apart from sampling issues, the telephone interviewer faces formidable challenges—finding the needed interviewees at home, dealing with interviewees who have been inundated with calls from telemarketers and vote solicitors, and thus are reluctant to talk.

Moreover, there is no assurance that persons interviewed will be truthful. Will people tell a stranger on the phone how they are going to vote? Will they answer demographic and sensitive personal profile questions that often are asked, such as income level? Will they tell the interviewer what they think the interviewer wants to hear? Despite these challenges Gallup and other major polling organizations have largely overcome them, learning through experience which strategies and protocols work, and training interviewers accordingly.

Lead Time of Surveys

Let us assume that survey methods are sound, and that we are dealing with trial heat polls that are accurate representations of voter preferences for candidates at the time the polls are taken. For forecasting purposes, the key question now becomes: When before an election do voters decide how they are going to vote? If we know that answer, polls taken at that time should be able to predict the election result.

In practice, the formation of voters' opinions of candidates is an evolving phenomenon, best viewed as a continuum. At points more remote in time from the election, fewer voters have decided how they will vote, and voters' opinions of the candidates may be fluid and unstable. Therefore, surveys made then presumably provide less accurate forecasts of the election. As the election nears, more voters make up their minds, with surveys made at later times producing progressively better election forecasts. But at what point will enough voters have made their voting decisions to permit an adequate election forecast?

At one extreme, the most accurate election forecasts are those based on surveys made at the time of the election. Indeed, exit polls conducted only minutes after people vote usually are very accurate. But such surveys are hardly useful as forecasts of voter behavior because they occur after the fact. Forecasts, by definition, occur *prior* to the event. Election forecasts must lead the election. But, on the other hand, if forecasts lead the election too far, when voter opinion is still fluid, they will lack accuracy. So, how much lead time for a survey can exist before the election and still result in a reasonably accurate forecast? How much forecast accuracy will be sacrificed for longer lead times, and how much accuracy will be gained by shorter lead times? An analysis of data, to which I now turn, can suggest answers.

Linking Surveys to Elections

Before studying the linkage of pre-election trial heat polls to election results, specific trial heats must be selected for analysis. It is important that surveys covering the long period since 1952 be comparable and use consistent and sound techniques. Thus, I rely on trial heats from only one organization, the highly regarded Gallup Poll. The dates within each month on which the Gallup organization conducted trial heats during this period varied from year to year. The polls included in this analysis are those made on the most similar monthly dates for the 13 election years studied. The average beginning and ending dates of the polls selected are:

> June 12–15
>
> July 17–21
>
> August 20–23
>
> September 21–24
>
> October 12–16
>
> October 30–November 2

Two means of linking polls to election outcomes will be considered: simple graphic comparison of trial heats with election results; and regression, a technique by which the ability of trial heats to account for election results can be determined statistically. For each approach I determine the strength of the relationship between the actual vote in November and trial heat polls made in preceding weeks and months, beginning in June and continuing until shortly before the November election. I thus follow the lead of political scientist James Campbell who, with a junior collaborator, was the first to explore these relationships in this way, after Lewis-Beck's earlier use of trial heats in a forecasting model (Campbell and Wink 1990; Campbell 1996; Lewis-Beck 1985, 58).

Graphic Comparisons

Simple graphic comparisons of each month's trial heat polls with presidential election results are presented in the six time-series line plots in Figure 1.1. In this figure, the solid line is the poll result, the number of respondents supporting the candidate of the incumbent president's party, as a percentage of all respondents favoring the Democratic and Republican candidates combined (thus eliminating support for other candidates from the total). The dashed line is the election result, similarly expressed as the percentage of the two-party vote garnered by the candidate of the incumbent president's party. Also, the 50 percent vote line, distinguishing wins from losses, is highlighted in the figure.

Not surprisingly, the line plots demonstrate that polls track election results better as time progresses, as the election nears. For the 1952–2000 period, the average percentage-point distance between the selected polls and the election result is highest in June, at 7.5 percent, and progressively drops to 2.1 percent in the final pre-election poll.

Suppose that we are concerned only with whether the polls made in the same month before the elections correctly identify election winners. For this purpose, we can observe in Figure 1.1 whether the results of a poll and of the election are on the same side of the 50 percent line. (For 2000, since Gore, the candidate of the incumbent party, garnered 50.3 percent of the two-party vote, this election is treated as a "win" for that party.)

Trial heats for the period selected in June and July incorrectly classified four election outcomes (in June: 1968, 1988, 1992, 2000; in July: 1960, 1984, 1988, 2000). Two elections were misclassified by the August polls (1952, 1980). September polls identified the winner in each election except one. In the latter (1980), the poll was inconclusive because the major party candidates both were favored by 50 percent of the respondents. October poll results are the strongest, with winners of the popular vote being correctly identified for all of the elections. Interestingly, the final pre-election polls did not perform as well, missing two election outcomes, the close finishes in 1976 and 2000.

Obviously, this is not a precise method for forecasting presidential election outcomes. At least one can say, based on recent history, that the major party candidate who is leading a trial heat in September or, especially, in October is likely to win the election. That assertion can be made with somewhat less confidence for August and November polls, and with much less confidence for June and July polls.

Focusing on recent elections, Figure 1.1 reveals that we could have predicted Clinton's victory in the one-sided 1996 contest by using any of the six monthly polls in this analysis, from June to November. All showed that Clinton had the support of more than 50 percent of those surveyed. In the 2000 campaign, poll results from June onward were variable, first with Bush leading, then Gore, and then Bush again in the home stretch. The final Gallup Poll favored Bush by two points, but Gore won the popular vote by 0.3 percent. Indeed, the last pre-election surveys of nearly all major polls favored Bush.

TRIAL HEATS AND ELECTION RESULTS, JUNE TO NOVEMBER

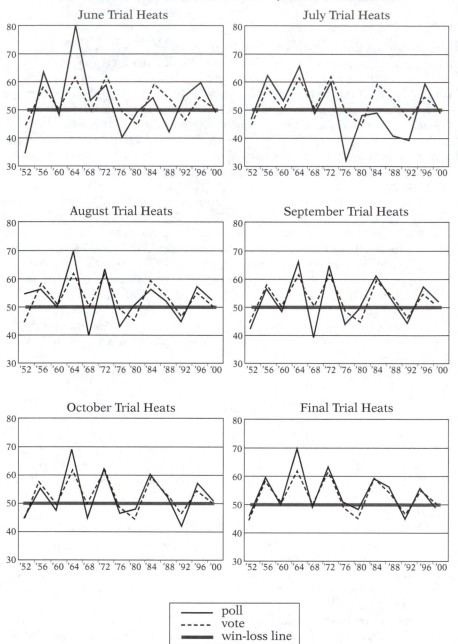

Figure 1.1

DATA SOURCES: Scammon, McGillivray, and Cook (1997)
Gallup (various entries listed in Bibliography)
U.S. Federal Election Commission (2001)

Data are incumbent party candidate's
share of two-party poll and election results.

Regression

The statistical technique of regression provides a more precise means of forecasting elections than does simple graphic comparison of trial heat polls and election results. Rather than merely indicating whether a candidate won or lost, regression produces a percentage forecast of a candidate's share of the vote. (See the appendix near the end of the book for a short description of regression, and the glossary of regression terms that follows it.)

In a simple two-variable regression, it is normally assumed that one phenomenon in the equation causes, or influences, the other. In this case, however, election results and trial heats both presumably are influenced by other factors not in the equation, and vary together for that reason. (Of course, it is possible that the relationship between trial heats and election outcomes exists in part because voters who want to be on the winning side are influenced in their voting choice by the results of trial heats—the bandwagon effect [Simon 1954].)

Among recent elections, the 1996 contest best illustrates the improved forecast accuracy of the regression approach, when compared to predictions based on trial heats alone. In the description that follows, the outcome of this election is linked by regression to the same monthly poll data—June to November—described in the preceding pages. The equations for the six months are reported in Table 1.1. Because the goal is to forecast the 1996 election, the election and poll data used in creating the equations end with the 1992 election.

Looking at Table 1.1, how should the information there be interpreted? Let us begin with "r^2," a statistic known as the "coefficient of determination." This is a useful measure of association between indicators, which in this case shows the extent that trial heats for a given month vary with election outcomes. Multiplying r^2 by 100 tells us, in essence, the percentage of the vote that is accounted for by the trial heats. As we see in the first column of numbers in Table 1.1, r^2 values are relatively high for trial heats in June, July,

Table 1.1 REGRESSIONS OF ELECTION RESULTS ON MONTHLY TRIAL HEATS, 1952–1992

Month	r^2	Adjusted r^2	Constant	Slope	t Value	Sig. of t Value	Durbin-Watson	Std. Error of Estimate
June	.49	.43	33.622	.359	2.926	.017	2.355	4.919
July	.44	.38	31.711	.421	2.664	.026	2.275	5.139
August	.53	.47	24.148	.542	3.164	.011	2.113	4.728
September	.80	.78	19.783	.633	6.060	.000	2.290	3.049
October	.85	.84	15.774	.704	7.211	.000	2.285	2.640
Final Poll	.91	.91	9.379	.798	9.806	.000	2.641	2.010

Number of cases (elections): 11
Dependent variable: share of two-party vote received by candidate of incumbent president's party.

Data Sources: Gallup (various entries listed in Bibliography); Scammon and McGillivray (1995).

and August, accounting for about half of the variation ("variance") in results for elections from 1952 to 1992. But between August and September the link between trial heats and election outcomes becomes significantly stronger, with the r^2 jumping from .53 to .80. That is, by the fourth week of September—six or seven weeks before the election—trial heats account for 80 percent of the election result. By the time of the final pre-election poll, a few days before the election, this figure rises to 91 percent.

To forecast an election outcome using the September regression equation, or equations for other months derived from Table 1.1, one merely inserts current trial heat data for that month into the appropriate equation. Suppose that in the fourth week of September in 1996 I had used the September equation to forecast that year's election result. The Gallup Poll interviews on September 21–23, 1996—dates close to the average historical dates in the regression data—showed Clinton preferred by 51 percent of the respondents, Dole by 38 percent, and Perot by 5 percent. ("Other" and "no opinion" responses were 6 percent [Gallup 1997, 134]). Since the equations are based on vote and poll results for the incumbent party's candidate as a share of the **two-party** total, I calculate Clinton's share of the combined Clinton and Dole "vote" in the September poll. That number, 57.3 percent, then is inserted into the September equation to obtain the predicted election outcome. As explained in the regression appendix, a regression equation has this form: The vote received by the incumbent party's candidate in the election is equal to the "constant" plus the "slope" times that candidate's share of the "vote" in the trial heat poll. Following this pattern, to predict the election result from the September trial heat, I use this equation taken from the September line in Table 1.1:

$$
\begin{aligned}
\text{incumbent (\textbf{Clinton}) share of two-party \textbf{vote} in \textbf{1996}} &= 19.783 + \left(.633 \times \begin{array}{l} \text{incumbent} \\ [\textbf{Clinton}] \text{ share} \\ \text{of } \textbf{September} \\ \text{two-party trial heats} \end{array} \right) \\
&= 19.783 + (.633 \times 57.3) \\
&= \textbf{56.1\%}
\end{aligned}
$$

EQUATION **1.1**

In the 1996 election, Clinton's share of the two-party vote was, in fact, 54.7 percent, a **difference (or error) of 1.4 percent** from the September forecast.

Let us now turn to Table 1.2. Column 4 in this table reports predictions of the 1996 election outcome produced by all six monthly equations, from June onward. We see in column 5 that the regression predictions all are within two percentage points of the election result, with the forecast error averaging only 1.0 percent. By contrast, column 3 reveals that trial heat polls were less successful in predicting the 1996 vote, with the forecast error averaging 3.1 percent.

This is a typical pattern, for in most elections regression forecasts derived from trial heats are more accurate predictors of election outcomes than actual

Table 1.2 1996 FORECASTS FOR CLINTON:
COMPARISON OF REGRESSION RESULTS AND RAW TRIAL HEAT DATA

(1) Trial Heat Month	(2) Trial Heat Result	(3) Trial Heat Error (col. 2 minus vote [54.7])	(4) Predictions from Trial Heat Regressions in Table 1.1	(5) Error in Regression Predictions (col. 4 minus vote [54.7])	(6) Margin of Error for Regression Predictions in col. 4
June	60.0%	**5.3%**	55.2%	**0.5%**	11.8%
July	59.4	**4.7**	56.7	**2.0**	12.7
August	56.8	**2.1**	54.9	**0.2**	11.3
September	57.3	**2.6**	56.1	**1.4**	7.3
October	57.3	**2.6**	56.1	**1.4**	6.3
Final Poll	55.9	**1.2**	54.0	**−0.7**	4.8
average forecast error:		**3.1**		**1.0**	

Trial heat and regression data are percent of two-party vote or two-party preferences in polls.
Regression equations are derived from 1952–1992 data, to produce 1996 forecasts.

Data Sources: Gallup (various entries listed in Bibliography); Scammon and McGillivray (1995).

trial heat results. This apparently was not the case, however, in 2000. As shown in Appendix 1.1, at the end of this chapter, five of the six polls identified for each month, June to November, were closer to the popular vote in 2000 than forecasts from regressions that used these data. Thus, the average forecast error for the trial heats was lower.

Although regression normally provides better predictions of election results than do trial heats alone, this approach is not without potential statistical problems when used for this purpose. A major concern is "autocorrelation." An explanation of this problem is beyond our purpose here, although the Glossary may be consulted for more information. Suffice it to say that, in this instance, evidence of autocorrelation would exist when the election outcomes are accounted for merely by the time sequence of trial heats in the successive elections in the data set. In essence, whatever shortcoming a trial heat might have in accounting for the vote in one election would be carried over to the next election. This problem can be detected by the Durbin-Watson test. Durbin-Watson scores reported in Table 1.1 all are within the acceptable range, indicating a 95 percent probability that no autocorrelation is present. (This test, too, is discussed in the Glossary.)

A second concern when forecasting elections with regression is the size of the forecast's confidence interval—sometimes called the forecast "margin of error." The confidence interval of a forecast defines the range within which a future election outcome is likely to occur, given that election's forecast. (The "standard error of the estimate," reported in Table 1.1, is important in calculating the confidence interval. Again, the Glossary provides a further explanation.) Forecasts produced by most regressions in this chapter will have wide confidence intervals, a significant shortcoming. Column 6 in Table 1.2

shows the extent to which the actual 1996 election result could have varied from the equation's forecast with a 95 percent probability. For the final trial heat equation, the 95 percent confidence limits for the 54 percent vote predicted for Clinton are +/− 4.8 percent. This margin of error becomes progressively greater for equations based on earlier trial heats, as evident in the table. (Also, the forecast margin of error associated with the equation for any given month would have been slightly different from that reported had different trial heat values been used in the equation. See Pindyck and Rubinfeld 1998, 208–209.) Of course, a major reason for the large margins of error is the small number of elections—11—used to generate the regression equations. Later we will find that when two or three variables are included in an equation, thereby improving its ability to fit the election data, the margin of error for resulting forecasts narrows.

The preceding election forecasts assume that we know the results of trial heat polls for the respective months in the election year and use that information to produce the forecasts. Thus, we are able to predict the election outcome using the September poll when that survey is conducted and reported in September, but not until then. If the poll results have not yet become available, forecasts using this approach cannot be made. However, alternative **scenarios** of possible election outcomes can be constructed, based on hypothetical values of Gallup Poll trial heats for September, or for the other months from June through early November.

Table 1.3 SCENARIOS FROM TRIAL HEATS:
THE DEMOCRATIC PRESIDENTIAL VOTE IN 2004

Two-Party "vote" for Democrat in Trial Heats in 2004	Two-Party Vote for Democrat in 2004 Election, Based on Trial Heat Results (in left column) for Month Indicated					
	June	July	Aug	Sept	Oct	Final Poll
60%	55.1	56.5	56.5	57.4	57.8	57.4
58	54.3	55.7	55.4	56.2	56.4	55.8
56	53.6	54.9	54.3	54.9	55.0	54.2
54	52.9	54.1	53.2	53.7	53.6	52.7
52	52.2	53.3	52.2	52.4	52.2	51.1
50	51.5	52.5	51.1	51.2	50.8	49.5
48	50.7	51.6	50.0	49.9	49.4	47.9
46	50.0	50.8	48.9	48.7	48.0	46.4
44	49.3	50.0	47.8	47.4	46.6	44.8
42	48.6	49.2	46.7	46.2	45.2	43.2
40	47.9	48.4	45.6	44.9	43.8	41.7

Example: An estimated October trial heat score of 56 percent for the Democrat results in a projection that the Democrat will receive 55.0 percent of the two-party vote in the election.

Computed from regression equations in Appendix 1.2 at the end of this chapter. Those equations are derived from 1952–2000 data.

Looking toward the 2004 election, suppose that we want to know how well the Democratic nominee would be expected to fare, if in September of that year the Gallup Poll were to report his support in trial heats as, say, 46 percent of the two-party "vote." To make this calculation, we first update the data set through the 2000 election, and then recalculate the September equation. The assumed poll figure of 46 percent for the Democrat is then entered into the equation to produce a conditional forecast for 2004, which is 48.7 percent of the two-party vote. Various scenarios can be calculated in this way, as reported for 2004 in Table 1.3. As evident in the table, one-sided trial heat results are moderated by the regression equations, especially in the earlier months. (The equations used in computing the scenarios for 2004, derived from 1952–2000 data, appear in Appendix 1.2 at the end of this chapter. Calculations for this example from the September equation are $19.835 + [.627 \times 46] = 48.7$.)

Conclusion

Even though criticizing trial heat polls is a popular activity in some quarters, campaign polls are, nevertheless, rather accurate predictors of presidential election outcomes. As early as six or seven weeks before an election—the fourth week in September—trial heats usually identify the winner correctly, and results improve further thereafter. Simple graphic comparison of trial heats with election results provide rather accurate predictions of the popular vote winners, but forecasts generated by regression equations have greater precision, predicting percentages of the vote. Moreover, regressions based on trial heats typically are more accurate election predictors than are the actual trial heat data, although the 2000 election appears to have been an exception to this pattern.

Margins of error for regression forecasts are large when the forecasts are based on trial heats prior to September. However, when forecasts are derived from polls for September and later, the margin of error drops to the 5–7 percent range. On balance, producing reasonably accurate forecasts six or seven weeks before an election seems to be a satisfactory compromise between forecast accuracy, on one hand, and the need for lead time sufficient for the forecast to be useful on the other.

Appendix 1.1
2000 Forecasts for Gore: Comparison of
Regression Results and Raw Trial Heat Data

(1) Trial Heat Month	(2) Trial Heat Result	(3) Trial Heat Error (col. 2 minus vote [50.3])	(4) Predictions from Trial Heat Regressions	(5) Error in Regression Predictions (col. 4 minus vote [50.3])	6) Margin of Error for Regression Predictions in col. 4
June	48.9%	−1.4%	51.1%	0.8%	10.9%
July	48.9	−1.4	52.2	1.9	11.4
August	52.2	1.9	52.4	2.1	10.4
September	51.7	1.4	52.4	2.1	6.8
October	50.6	0.3	51.3	1.0	5.9
Final Poll	48.9	−1.4	48.4	−1.9	4.6
average forecast error:		1.3		1.6	

Trial heat and regression data are percent of two-party vote or two-party preferences in polls.
Regression equations are derived from 1952–1996 data to produce 2000 forecasts.

Data Sources: Gallup (various entries listed in Bibliography); Scammon, McGillivray, and Cook (1997);
U.S. Federal Election Commission (2001).

Appendix 1.2
Trial Heat Equations for 2004 Election
Scenarios, 1952–2000 Data

Hypothetical forecast scenarios for the 2004 presidential election, appearing
in Table 1.3, were generated by inserting trial heat poll data for a given month
into the equation for that month, as follows. In 2004, readers can easily calculate their own forecasts by dropping the poll results for the Democratic
candidate for the appropriate time periods into these equations. (Recall that
we are concerned with the Democrat's percentage of the Democratic and
Republican total in the poll, omitting other candidates.) Ideally, trial heats
should be from the time period within the month that was used in the historical data from which the equations were created. Those dates are listed in this
chapter.

June

$$\text{incumbent (Dem.) share of two-party vote in 2004} = 33.494 + \left(.359 \times \text{incumbent [Dem.] share of June 2004 two-party trial heats} \right)$$

r^2 .50 (.45 adjusted)   Durbin-Watson score 2.531
t-value 3.300   standard error of estimate 4.458
  (significance .01)

July

$$\begin{matrix} \text{incumbent (Dem.)} \\ \text{share of two-party} \\ \textbf{vote} \text{ in } \textbf{2004} \end{matrix} = 32.071 + \left(.408 \times \begin{matrix} \text{incumbent [Dem.]} \\ \text{share of } \textbf{July 2004} \\ \text{two-party trial heats} \end{matrix} \right)$$

r^2 .44 (.39 adjusted)   Durbin-Watson score 2.245
t-value 2.932   standard error of estimate 4.712
  (significance .01)

August

$$\begin{matrix} \text{incumbent (Dem.)} \\ \text{share of two-party} \\ \textbf{vote} \text{ in } \textbf{2004} \end{matrix} = 23.938 + \left(.543 \times \begin{matrix} \text{incumbent [Dem.]} \\ \text{share of } \textbf{August 2004} \\ \text{two-party trial heats} \end{matrix} \right)$$

r^2 .53 (.49 adjusted)   Durbin-Watson score 2.101
t-value 3.506   standard error of estimate 4.322
  (significance .00)

September

$$\begin{matrix} \text{incumbent (Dem.)} \\ \text{share of two-party} \\ \textbf{vote} \text{ in } \textbf{2004} \end{matrix} = 19.835 + \left(.627 \times \begin{matrix} \text{incumbent [Dem.]} \\ \text{share of } \textbf{Sept 2004} \\ \text{two-party trial heats} \end{matrix} \right)$$

r^2 .80 (.78 adjusted)Durbin-Watson score 2.142
t-value 6.525   standard error of estimate 2.850
  (significance .00)

October

$$\begin{matrix} \text{incumbent (Dem.)} \\ \text{share of two-party} \\ \textbf{vote} \text{ in } \textbf{2004} \end{matrix} = 15.896 + \left(.698 \times \begin{matrix} \text{incumbent [Dem.]} \\ \text{share of } \textbf{October 2004} \\ \text{two-party trial heats} \end{matrix} \right)$$

r^2 .85 (.84 adjusted)   Durbin-Watson score 2.285
t-value 7.884   standard error of estimate 2.438
  (significance .00)

Final Poll (late October–early November)

$$\begin{matrix} \text{incumbent (Dem.)} \\ \text{share of two-party} \\ \textbf{vote} \text{ in } \textbf{2004} \end{matrix} = 10.237 + \left(.785 \times \begin{matrix} \text{incumbent [Dem.]} \\ \text{share of } \textbf{Final 2004} \\ \text{two-party trial heats} \end{matrix} \right)$$

r^2 .91 (.90 adjusted)   Durbin-Watson score 2.425
t-value 10.443   standard error of estimate 1.903
  (significance .00)

Equations are based on data for 13 election years, 1952–2000.

The Democrat is treated as the "incumbent" in 2004 because Democrat Gore won the popular vote in 2000. Alternatively, 2004 data for the Republican could be entered into these equations to predict the 2004 Republican vote.

Data Sources: Gallup (various entries listed in Bibliography); Scammon, McGillivray, and Cook (1997); U.S. Federal Election Commission (2001).

Bellwethers

As Maine goes, so goes the Nation.

traditional campaign slogan

As Maine goes, so goes Vermont!

1936 revision, when only Maine and Vermont voted Republican

As Delaware goes, so goes the Nation.

a slogan for today, accurate since 1952

In the preceding chapter, I described techniques of predicting presidential election results based on surveys in which prospective voters are asked their candidate preferences. In this chapter, a variation of this approach is considered. Rather than focusing on the national level, I identify smaller electoral units—states and counties—that have voting patterns similar to those of the nation as a whole, that are electoral microcosms of the nation. If voter opinion in these subdivisions, or "bellwethers," reflects opinion in the nation, it should be possible to forecast the national vote from election results or surveys in the bellwethers.

To forecast a presidential election a month or two before the balloting, one can use surveys of likely voters in the bellwether in which people there are asked their voting intentions. For election night forecasts, the early results of exit polls or actual election results of bellwethers in the Eastern time zone can provide several hours lead time in identifying the national election winner.

In this chapter, we are concerned primarily with bellwether states and, to a lesser extent, with bellwether counties. In first approaching the subject, three generic types of bellwethers will be described. Then the most promising bellwether states will be identified and their usefulness in forecasting the national presidential vote demonstrated. The chapter concludes with an evaluation of counties as national electoral bellwethers, giving particular attention to a county in Ohio, a strong bellwether state.

Types of Bellwethers

In past electoral studies, the term "bellwether" often has been used in three ways, as identified by Yale political scientist Edward Tufte and his collaborator, Richard Sun (Tufte 1974, 46–54; Tufte and Sun 1975). First, "bellwether" may refer to electoral subdivisions—states and counties, for our purposes—that over time have voted consistently for the winners in presidential elections. Tufte and Sun call these **all-or-nothing** bellwethers. When the term is used in this way, the concern is not whether the vote of the state or county is of the same magnitude as the national vote, merely whether it is in the same direction. This is a dichotomous classification: The state or county either votes for the winner or it does not.

A second use of the term refers to states or counties whose votes for president vary consistently with the national vote. The bellwether's vote may closely mirror the magnitude of the national vote, or it may be many percentage points away from it and may not even favor the winner. But in any case, as pioneer election forecaster Louis Bean, a specialist in the use of bellwethers, noted: "the two patterns [state and national] tend to rise and fall together . . . with fairly consistent margins between them" (Bean 1948, 106). If, for example, a state votes 10 percent more Democratic than the nation as a whole, but does so consistently in election after election, one can forecast the national Democratic vote from the state vote by subtracting 10 percent from the vote expected in the state for the Democrat in the next election. Tufte and Sun label these bellwethers **swingometric**.

A third type identified by Tufte and Sun are **barometric** bellwethers. These are states or counties the votes of which closely mirror the national vote. In some elections, a barometric bellwether's percentage vote for a candidate may be a bit higher than that for the nation as a whole, and in other elections, it may be a bit lower. In each election, however, the percentage vote in the barometric bellwether will be close to that of the nation.

States: All-or-Nothing Bellwethers

Which states are good bellwethers of the national vote for president? First, let us look at all-or-nothing bellwethers, states that reveal the national winner regardless of how close the state outcomes are to the national result. Traditionally, Maine was considered an all-or-nothing bellwether. Until 1960, its gubernatorial elections were held in September of even-numbered years, two months before presidential elections. When in 1840 the Maine vote for a Whig governor presaged the national vote for a Whig president, the slogan was born "As Maine goes, so goes the nation" (Palmer, Taylor, and LiBrizzi 1992, 148–149). This slogan was accurate only about two-thirds of the time, but lived on until 1936 when only Maine and Vermont voted Republican in the Democratic landslide for Roosevelt. James Farley, Roosevelt's campaign manager, responded with his own revision of the slogan: "As Maine goes, so goes Vermont!" (Tufte 1974, 47).

For our purposes, we are concerned with the extent to which candidates for president win both in a given state and in the nation. Suppose we choose the 84-year period, 1916–2000. Are there any states that have voted for the winners in each presidential election since then? (For the 2000 election, I assume that the winner of the popular vote is the "election winner.") Table 2.1 gives the state-by-state results; an "X" in the table identifies a state that did *not* vote for the winner in the election indicated. As seen in the table, not even one state voted for the winner in all of these elections. New Mexico has the best record; it failed to support the victor only in 1976 (Congressional Quarterly 1997, 84; Petersen 1968, 166–168; U.S. Federal Election Commission 2001).

If we use a shorter and more recent period, covering elections from 1952 to 2000, the results are better. Delaware has voted for the winner in every election since 1952. But it is the only state that has done so. Four states have voted for the winner in all but one election: Illinois, New Jersey, New Mexico, and Pennsylvania. In short, Delaware is the best all-or-nothing bellwether state for recent presidential elections. As Delaware goes, so goes the nation!

States: Swingometric and Barometric Bellwethers

Let us now consider swingometric and barometric bellwether states. Recall that the vote of a swingometric bellwether varies consistently and at a constant interval above the national vote or below it; the vote of a barometric bellwether is close to the national vote and may be above it in one election and below it in another.

For states to qualify as swingometric or barometric bellwethers they should have voting patterns that are highly associated with the national vote. Patterns of association can be identified by calculating r^2 for each state-nation pair, which in this case measures the proportion of variation in the national vote that can be accounted for by the variation in a state's vote. Regression facilitates forecasting by providing a precise means of relating the bellwether's vote to that of the nation (as Meier [1979] has demonstrated with county bellwethers of a state's vote).

Table 2.2 reports the extent that election results for individual states vary with election results for the nation. Data in the table are for the 12 elections from 1952 through 1996 for the 48 states that existed throughout that period. For seven state-nation relationships, the bellwether state can account for 90 percent or more of the variation in the national vote, evident from their "common variation" values printed in italics in the table. (These are r^2 values times 100. See the Glossary for details.) For each of the seven, the national vote has been linked separately to the state vote. The key elements of each state's regression equation—the constant and slope—are reported in Table 2.3 along with other relevant data. Durbin-Watson scores shown in the table indicate that autocorrelation is not a problem for six of the seven equations. It might be a problem, however, for Indiana since results for the test are inconclusive. U.S. forecasts from the Indiana equation thus have less reliability than those from the other six bellwethers in the table.

We know from Table 2.3 that three of the bellwether states can account for 94 percent or more of the variation in the national vote (r^2 times 100), with standard errors of the estimate less than 1.7, certain to result in low forecast confidence intervals—no more than $+/-4$ percent. These states are Pennsylvania, Ohio, and Indiana, contiguous states that in the past have been at or near the geographic center of population of the country (U.S. Bureau of the Census 1996, 27).

Swingometric Indiana and Pennsylvania

Indiana clearly is a swingometric bellwether, and a good case can be made that Pennsylvania is too. (Recall that swingometric bellwethers are states whose voting patterns are either all higher than the national vote, or all lower, and parallel to it.) In Figure 2.1, it is evident that Indiana's vote tracks the national vote well, even though it is more Republican than the nation. The important characteristic is that Indiana is *consistently* more Republican.

By contrast, Pennsylvania is less Republican—more Democratic—than the nation as a whole, as also evident in Figure 2.1. The gap over time between its vote and the national vote is not as wide as that for Indiana and the nation. The difference between Pennsylvania and the nation, however, is sufficiently consistent to also produce a close relationship between the two statistically.

To predict the national vote, one inserts the bellwether's actual or estimated vote into the appropriate regression equation. Using the Pennsylvania and Indiana equations from Table 2.3, we can generate forecasts of the 2000 election based on these swingometric bellwethers. To illustrate, the actual two-party state election results for 2000 are used: 47.852 percent for Bush in Pennsylvania and 58.005 percent for Bush in Indiana (U.S. Federal Election Commission 2001). (Three decimal places are used for these data to add precision in predicting this close election, after the fact.) Substituting these data into the appropriate equations produces these results:

for Pennsylvania

$$\text{Rep. (\textbf{Bush}) share of two-party \textbf{U.S.} vote in \textbf{2000}} = 3.602 + \left(.969 \times \begin{array}{l} \text{Rep. (\textbf{Bush}) share} \\ \text{of two-party} \\ \textbf{Penn.}\text{ vote in \textbf{2000}} \end{array} \right)$$

$$= 3.602 + (.969 \times 47.852)$$

$$= \mathbf{49.97\%}$$

EQUATION 2.1

for Indiana

$$\text{Rep. (\textbf{Bush}) share of two-party \textbf{U.S.} vote in \textbf{2000}} = -11.781 + \left(1.118 \times \begin{array}{l} \text{Rep. (\textbf{Bush}) share} \\ \text{of two-party} \\ \textbf{Indiana}\text{ vote in \textbf{2000}} \end{array} \right)$$

$$= -11.781 + (1.118 \times 58.005)$$

$$= \mathbf{53.07\%}$$

EQUATION 2.2

In the 2000 election, Bush received 49.73 percent of the two-party national vote. This was **a mere 0.24 percent lower** than the Pennsylvania

Table 2.1 STATES *NOT* VOTING FOR WINNER OF POPULAR VOTE IN PRESIDENTIAL ELECTIONS, 1916–2000

	16	20	24	28	32	36	40	44	48	52	56	60	64	68	72	76	80	84	88	92	96	00
Alabama		X	X	X					X	X	X	X	X	X						X	X	X
Arizona		X	X						X			X	X							X	X	X
Arkansas			X	X						X	X			X		X						X
California							X	X				X		X		X						X
Colorado							X	X				X				X					X	X
Connecticut	X				X	X			X					X							X	X
Delaware	X				X				X													X
Florida		X	X							X		X		X		X				X	X	X
Georgia		X	X	X						X	X	X	X	X		X	X			X	X	X
Idaho	X											X				X						X
Illinois	X						X	X	X			X		X		X				X	X	X
Indiana	X				X	X	X	X	X			X		X		X				X	X	X
Iowa	X				X		X	X	X	X		X		X	X	X			X	X	X	X
Kansas						X	X	X	X			X		X		X						
Kentucky		X								X			X	X								
Louisiana		X	X	X					X	X		X	X	X		X						
Maine	X				X	X	X	X	X			X	X	X		X				X	X	X
Maryland														X			X					
Massachusetts	X			X										X	X				X			
Michigan	X						X		X					X		X						
Minnesota	X																	X	X			
Mississippi		X	X	X			X		X	X		X	X			X	X	X		X	X	X
Missouri											X											
Montana												X				X				X	X	X
Nebraska		X	X				X	X				X				X		X		X	X	X
Nevada									X							X						X

New Hampshire				X							X		
New Jersey	X			X			X				X	X	X
New Mexico	X						X					X	X
New York	X	X		X			X			X		X	X
N. Carolina		X	X	X	X		X	X			X	X	X
N. Dakota			X				X				X	X	X
Ohio		X					X				X	X	X
Oklahoma	X			X			X	X		X	X	X	X
Oregon	X	X		X	X		X				X	X	X
Pennsylvania	X	X	X				X				X	X	X
Rhode Island						X							X
S. Carolina	X	X		X	X		X			X	X	X	X
S. Dakota	X			X	X	X	X				X	X	X
Tennessee	X	X								X			X
Texas	X	X								X			X
Utah				X			X				X	X	X
Vermont	X		X	X	X	X	X				X	X	X
Virginia	X	X					X				X	X	X
Washington							X	X				X	X
W. Virginia	X				X		X	X	X	X	X	X	X
Wisconsin	X	X			X		X				X	X	X
Wyoming	X			X	X		X				X	X	X

X = state failed to vote for winner of popular vote

States in italics have voted for the winner in all elections, or all but one, since 1952.

Sources: Adapted from Svend Petersen, *A Statistical History of the American Presidential Elections* (New York: Frederick Ungar Publishing Co., 1968), p. 167. Additional data from Congressional Quarterly (1997, 84) and U.S. Federal Election Commission (2001).

Table 2.2 ASSOCIATION BETWEEN STATE AND NATIONAL ELECTION RESULTS, 1952–1996

State	% Common Variation	State	% Common Variation
Alabama	11%	Nebraska	77%
Arizona	74	Nevada	78
Arkansas	50	*New Hampshire*	*90*
California	82	*New Jersey*	*92*
Colorado	88	New Mexico	89
Connecticut	89	New York	87
Delaware	*90*	North Carolina	40
Florida	72	North Dakota	64
Georgia	3	*Ohio*	*95*
Idaho	66	Oklahoma	65
Illinois	86	Oregon	72
Indiana	*94*	*Pennsylvania*	*95*
Iowa	57	Rhode Island	84
Kansas	77	South Carolina	2
Kentucky	77	South Dakota	44
Louisiana	27	Tennessee	49
Maine	76	Texas	80
Maryland	89	Utah	56
Massachusetts	73	Vermont	66
Michigan	89	Virginia	85
Minnesota	78	Washington	87
Mississippi	4	*West Virginia*	*91*
Missouri	86	Wisconsin	70
Montana	80	Wyoming	80

The "percent [of] common variation" is r^2, the coefficient of determination, multiplied by 100. This is a measure of the strength of association between elections in each state and national elections: 100 is a perfect relationship; zero is no relationship whatever.
Italicized are states with values of 90 or higher (i.e., r^2 of .90 +).
All election data are Republican candidates' share of the two-party vote.

Data Source: Scammon, McGillivray, and Cook (1997).

equation's forecast of 49.97 percent and, of course, well within the +/− 3.5 percent margin of error. The Indiana forecast was less successful, predicting 53.07 percent for Bush. This prediction was 3.34 percent higher than Bush's national vote, though within the 3.9 percent confidence interval.

While the regression approach is the most precise way to forecast with swingometric bellwethers, a simpler and more approximate approach also is possible. As mentioned previously, if we know how a swingometric bellwether state is going to vote, and if its vote parallels the national vote, then we should be able to forecast the national vote by observing the gap between the bellwether state and nation over a selected historical period. The average "distance" between votes of the bellwether and nation can be calculated, and that average would be the forecast gap between the bellwether's vote and the national vote in the upcoming election.

Table 2.3 REGRESSIONS OF U.S. REPUBLICAN VOTE ON REPUBLICAN VOTE IN STRONGEST BELLWETHER STATES, 1952–1996

State	r^2	Adjusted r^2	Constant	Slope	t Value	Durbin-Watson	Standard Error of Estimate
Delaware	.91	.89	5.237	0.921	9.704	1.415	2.138
Indiana	.94	.94	−11.781	1.118	12.777	1.163	1.658
New Hampshire	.90	.89	16.559	0.620	9.688	2.076	2.141
New Jersey	.92	.91	15.478	0.689	10.860	2.585	1.929
Ohio	.96	.95	2.634	0.929	14.588	1.804	1.462
Pennsylvania	.95	.95	3.602	0.969	13.975	1.762	1.523
West Virginia	.91	.90	14.867	0.785	9.828	1.363	2.113

t-values are significant at the .00 level.
Election data are of the two-party vote.
Equations are based on data for 12 elections, 1952–1996.

Data Source: Scammon, McGillivray, and Cook (1997).

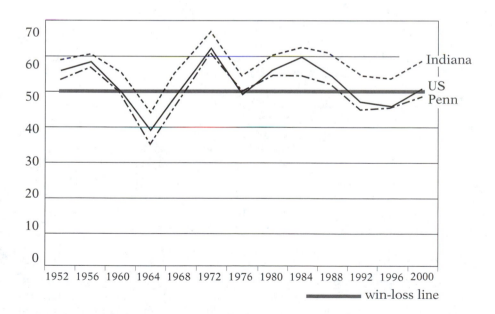

TWO SWINGOMETRIC BELLWETHER STATES:
TWO-PARTY REPUBLICAN VOTE IN
INDIANA AND PENNSYLVANIA

Figure 2.1

DATA SOURCES: Scammon, McGillivray, and Cook (1997)
U.S. Federal Election Commission (2001)

Table 2.4 DIFFERENCE BETWEEN REPUBLICAN VOTES IN TWO SWINGOMETRIC
BELLWETHERS AND IN UNITED STATES

	Indiana Vote % Rep.	Penn. Vote % Rep.	US Vote % Rep.	Indiana Minus US	Penn. Minus US
1952	58.6	53.0	55.4	3.2	−2.4
1956	60.1	56.6	57.8	2.3	−1.2
1960	55.2	48.8	49.9	5.3	−1.1
1964	43.8	34.8	38.7	5.1	−3.9
1968	57.0	48.1	50.4	6.6	−2.3
1972	66.5	60.2	61.8	4.7	−1.6
1976	53.8	48.6	48.9	4.9	−0.3
1980	59.8	53.9	55.3	4.5	−1.4
1984	62.1	53.7	59.2	2.9	−5.5
1988	60.1	51.2	53.9	6.2	−2.7
1992	53.8	44.5	46.5	7.3	−2.0
1996	58.0	47.9	49.7	8.3	−1.8
average:				**+5.1**	**−2.2**

All election data are of the two-party vote.
Data Source: Scammon, McGillivray, and Cook (1997).

As seen in Table 2.4, for Indiana the average gap between its vote and the national vote, for 1952–1996, was +5.1 percent. That is, the Indiana vote on average was 5.1 percent more Republican than that of the nation. For Pennsylvania, this distance was −2.2 percent, the negative value reflecting its tendency to vote less Republican (more Democratic) than the country as a whole.

To forecast the Republican vote in the 2000 national election, one merely subtracts 5.1 percent from the estimate of the 2000 Indiana vote or adds 2.2 percent to the 2000 estimated vote for Pennsylvania. To illustrate, I again use the actual 2000 Republican share of the two-party vote in these states: 58.0 percent for Indiana and 47.9 percent for Pennsylvania. For Indiana data, this procedure yields a forecast for Bush of 52.9 percent of the national vote (58.0 minus 5.1). With Pennsylvania data, the comparable forecast is 50.1 percent (47.9 plus 2.2). Since Bush actually received 49.7 percent of the two-party national vote, the errors in the national forecasts are 3.2 percent for Indiana data and only 0.4 percent for Pennsylvania data.

Barometric Ohio

Ohio is the best example of a barometric bellwether state. Its vote is historically very close to the national vote. As evident in Figure 2.2, Ohio sometimes has voted slightly less Republican than the nation, more often a bit more Republican, and sometimes with percentages virtually identical to the national vote. To illustrate forecasting with barometric bellwethers, I use the 2000 vote in Ohio to predict the national 2000 vote. The two-party Ohio elec-

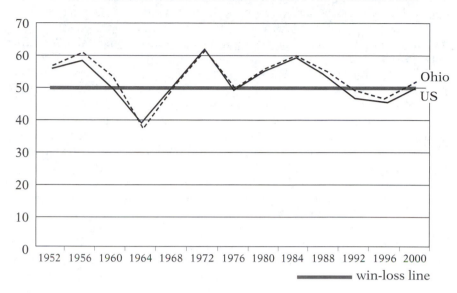

OHIO BAROMETRIC BELLWETHER: TWO-PARTY REPUBLICAN VOTE

Figure 2.2

DATA SOURCES: McGillivray and Cook (1997)
            U.S. Federal Election Commission (2001)

tion results (51.839 percent for Bush) are substituted into the following equation, taken from Table 2.3 and based on 1952–1996 data:

$$
\begin{aligned}
\text{Rep. (\textbf{Bush}) share of two-party \textbf{U.S.} vote in \textbf{2000}} &= 2.634 + \left(.929 \times \text{Rep. (\textbf{Bush}) share of two-party \textbf{Ohio} vote in \textbf{2000}}\right) \\
&= 2.634 + (.929 \times 51.839) \\
&= 50.79\%
\end{aligned}
$$

EQUATION 2.3

The margin of error for this forecast is +/− 3.4 percent, with a 95 percent probability. Since Bush actually received 49.73 percent of the national two-party vote, this prediction (50.79%) is **off only 1.1 percent,** well within the margin of error.

Predicting a Bellwether State's Vote: Pennsylvania

Thus far in illustrating forecasting techniques based on swingometric and barometric bellwethers, I have used state election *results* to forecast the national election outcome. This approach can produce forecasts on election night after votes in the bellwether have been counted. The examples used in the previous discussion are states in the Eastern time zone. Since these state results presumably are available early on election night, they potentially could predict the national election outcome a few hours before it is available, before polls close in other time zones.

Perhaps a more useful approach is to use the results of *exit polls* in Eastern states, which can provide more hours of lead time for forecasts of the national vote. The Voter News Service, jointly supported by television networks and other media, conducts state-by-state exit polls that normally are aired when a state's polls close. One could insert exit poll results for a strong bellwether state into that state's regression of the national vote, producing a national vote estimate when the state's exit poll results become available.

For example, the Cable News Network exit poll for Pennsylvania in 2000 indicated that Bush would receive 47.9 percent of the two-party vote in Pennsylvania, a result remarkably close to the actual vote (calculated from data in Cable News Network 2000b). This information was available for broadcast shortly after the polls closed at 8:00 P.M. Eastern time. Substituting the Pennsylvania exit poll results for Bush into equation 2.1 (U.S.-Pennsylvania), Bush would have been forecast to receive 50.0 percent of the national vote, only 0.3 percent more than his actual two-party vote, and well within the forecast's 3.5 percent margin of error in the equation. (Of course, the poll's margin of error should be considered, too.)

State exit polls or actual state vote results do not, of course, forecast how people will vote in a future election. Rather, they provide early estimates of the outcome of an election that has already occurred, earlier that day. Their use accelerates reporting the results of a prior event.

To make national forecasts using bellwethers with lead time before an election—that is, true *ex ante* forecasts—we need access to *forecasts of the state vote*. The results of these trial heat polls in the bellwether can then be inserted into the regression equation linking that state to the national vote. To illustrate, I again use Pennsylvania as the bellwether.

During the 2000 pre-election campaign, several polling organizations conducted trial heat surveys in Pennsylvania. Among the most accurate was Mason-Dixon Polling and Research in Washington, D.C. A Mason-Dixon poll in September showed 45 percent of the Pennsylvania electorate favoring Gore, 41 percent for Bush, 4 percent for others, and 10 percent undecided (Mason-Dixon 2000). Of those supporting only Gore and Bush, Bush was preferred by 47.7 percent. If that figure for Bush is inserted into the equation for Pennsylvania, the result predicts Bush receiving 49.8 percent of the national two-party vote. Given that Bush in fact garnered 49.7 percent, this prediction of the national election outcome, based on a September poll in Pennsylvania, is nearly perfect with an **error of only 0.1 percent**.

The final Mason-Dixon poll in Pennsylvania before the election gave Gore 48 percent, Bush 45 percent, others 2 percent, with 5 percent undecided (Mason-Dixon 2000). Bush's share of the two-party "vote" in this survey was 48.4 percent. Using this figure, the Pennsylvania equation predicts Bush receiving 50.5 percent of the national two-party vote, a slightly less accurate forecast, **0.8 percent in error**.

We see from this use of trial heat surveys in Pennsylvania that it is possible to predict, rather accurately, the outcome of a presidential election with poll results from a bellwether state. However, accuracy of the national forecasts is very much dependent on the quality of the state poll selected, the timing of the survey, and, of course, the strength of the relationship between the state and national voting patterns evident in the regression equation.

Counties as Bellwethers

I now turn to bellwether counties, though with less confidence than when dealing with bellwether states. Most states are large enough potentially to be national microcosms—to include the variety of electoral and demographic characteristics that exist in the nation. Because of their size, subdivisions as small as most counties are less likely to be electoral microcosms of the nation, even though they may have reflected the national vote historically. Any relationship between their voting patterns and that of the nation may well be due largely to chance.

These concerns can be raised with regard to counties identified as bellwethers by Tufte and Sun (1975) in an ambitious study of the 3000-plus counties in the nation. They found that Palo Alto county, Iowa; Crook county, Oregon; and Laramie county, Wyoming, sided with the winner in presidential elections from 1916 through 1968. These counties are small and mostly rural. (The capital of Wyoming, Cheyenne, is in Laramie county.) They lack the diverse mix of demographic and other characteristics evident nationally. Voters in the 2000 presidential election numbered only 4823 in Palo Alto county, 8259 in Crook county, and 34,715 in Laramie county. Indeed, since 1972 the performance of the three counties as bellwethers has suffered. Through 1996, Palo Alto and Crook counties failed to side with the presidential winner in two elections, and Laramie county missed three. All three went for Bush in 2000, though Palo Alto was very close, with 50.2 percent of the two-party vote. Regressions of the national vote on the vote in those counties, using 1952–1996 data, produced r^2 values of .74 for Laramie, .54 for Crook, and .43 for Palo Alto. This means that these counties can account for 74 percent, 54 percent, and 43 percent of variation in the national vote, respectively—hardly impressive, especially for Crook and Palo Alto counties.

In 1996, the *New York Times* featured another county as a promising presidential bellwether, Stark county, Ohio, located in the northeast part of that state south of Akron and Cleveland. (The series of *Times* articles on Stark county is available on the Web at **http://www.nytimes.com/specials/canton/**.) In a state that is itself a strong bellwether, voters in Stark county have sided with the winner of the national popular vote in five of the last six elections, through 2000. Even though Stark county has been a good all-or-nothing bellwether since 1980, it has voted somewhat more Republican than the nation as a whole, particularly prior to 1980. For the 1952–1996 period,

Stark county still is a strong bellwether, given its 95 percent variation with the national vote, which is higher than for any other county in Ohio. However, since Stark county votes more Republican than the nation—failing to side with the national winner in two elections during this time—it is best classified as a swingometric bellwether for the entire period.

Regressing the national vote on the Stark county vote for 1952–1996 produced the following equation, which can be used to forecast the 2000 national vote. When the two-party Stark county vote for Republican Bush (51.012%), is substituted into the equation, these are the results:

$$\text{Rep. (\textbf{Bush}) share of two-party \textbf{U.S.} vote in \textbf{2000}} = 7.542 + .819 \times \left(\begin{array}{c} \text{Rep. (\textbf{Bush}) share} \\ \text{of two-party \textbf{Stark}} \\ \textbf{County} \text{ vote in \textbf{2000}} \end{array} \right)$$

$$= 7.542 + (.819 \times 51.012)$$

$$= \textbf{49.32\%}$$

EQUATION 2.4

r^2 .95 (.94 adjusted)	Durbin-Watson score 2.087
t-value 13.576	standard error of the estimate 1.565
(significance .00)	number of elections 12 (1952–1996)

Given that Bush received 49.73 percent of the national two-party vote, the Stark county prediction of 49.32 percent is **off only 0.4 percent**, well within the $+/-$ 3.7 percent margin of error.

The success of Stark county as a national bellwether is not surprising. It is larger than the three counties identified earlier; more than 150,000 persons voted for president in 2000. Moreover, it seems more representative of the nation, with Canton, the county seat, being the site of the professional football Hall of Fame and the home of a president, William McKinley.

Scenarios Using Bellwethers

Suppose that before a presidential election we want to know how well a candidate would need to perform in a bellwether in order to win the national election. One way to do this is to calculate scenarios of possible national outcomes, given various election results in the bellwether. Illustrate this approach with scenarios for the 2004 election, based on hypothetical values for the Republican candidate's standing in selected bellwethers. To create the 2004 scenarios, the regression equations for the seven states in Table 2.3 were recomputed using updated 1952–2000 data. In these equations, two states—Ohio and Pennsylvania—accounted for 95 percent of the variation in the national vote. Stark County, Ohio, did so as well. Thus, these were selected for the 2004 scenarios. The equations for them appear in Appendix 2.1 at the end of this chapter.

The forecast scenarios for 2004 are reported in Table 2.5. Suppose, for example, that the Republican candidate were to receive 54 percent of the two-party "vote" in a trial heat poll in Ohio. In that case, as we see in the table,

Table 2.5 SCENARIOS FROM BELLWETHERS:
UNITED STATES VOTE FOR PRESIDENT IN 2004 ELECTION

Two-Party Vote for Republican in Bellwether	National Two-Party Vote for Republican Based on Vote in Bellwether (specified in the first column)		
	Ohio	Pennsylvania	Stark County, Ohio
60%	58.3%	61.8%	56.7%
58	56.5	59.8	55.1
56	54.6	57.9	53.4
54	52.7	55.9	51.8
52	50.9	54.0	50.2
50	49.0	52.1	48.5
48	47.2	50.1	46.9
46	45.3	48.2	45.3
44	43.4	46.2	43.6
42	41.6	44.3	42.0
40	39.7	42.3	40.4

Example: If the two-party vote for the Republican candidate in Pennsylvania were 52%, then the two-party national vote for that candidate would be projected at 54.0%.

Calculations are derived from equations in Appendix 2.1. Data are for 1952–2000.

the Republican would be expected to garner 52.7 percent of the national two-party vote. (Calculations using the Ohio equation are in Appendix 2.1: $2.428 + [.932 \times 54] = 52.7$.)

Conclusion

In this chapter, we have seen that the presidential vote in some states and counties is strongly linked to the national vote for president. The vote in some (all-or-nothing bellwethers) consistently sides with the national winner; the vote in others (barometric bellwethers) is invariably close to the national vote, whether slightly above or slightly below it; the vote in still others (swingo-metric bellwethers) varies in tandem with the national vote, though a gap of several percentage points exists between the two. Any of these bellwethers potentially can provide an accurate forecast of the national vote if it leads the national vote in time (as with states in the Eastern time zone on election night) or if trial heat surveys in the bellwether are available.

When a state or county mirrors and can predict the national vote, it easily captures journalists' attention and the popular imagination. As national forecasting devices, however, bellwethers likely are less efficient than other approaches. For example, if the goal is to forecast the national vote, why not use a national trial heat poll rather than a state trial heat in a bellwether state? National polls by reputable survey organizations are readily available during the weeks and months before the election. State polls in bellwether states, like Pennsylvania, usually are available less frequently. Moreover, typical state polls have smaller samples than national polls. Yet, as we know from statisticians, smaller samples are not more justifiable for states than for the nation merely because state populations are smaller. The error in smaller-sample state polls is likely to be greater than in larger-sample national polls.

Also, sufficiently long historical series of state trial heat polling data, needed for developing regressions of the national vote, likely are not available for most states. Thus, the regression equations are derived from actual state election data rather than state trial heats. Less forecast error likely would exist if we had state trial heat data since 1952, which we have for the nation.

On balance, bellwethers are interesting, but better methods exist for forecasting the national vote in presidential elections.

Appendix 2.1
Bellwether Equations for 2004 Election Scenarios, 1952–2000 Data

In 2004, the reader can use these equations to predict the national vote from state polls or from early returns on election night.

Ohio Equation

Rep. share of two-party **U.S.** vote in **2004** = 2.428 + (.932 × Rep. share of two-party **Ohio** vote in **2004**)

r^2 .95 (.95 adjusted)   Durbin-Watson score 1.739
t-value 14.988   standard error of the estimate 1.428
(significance .00)

Pennsylvania Equation

Rep. share of two-party **U.S.** vote in **2004** = 3.515 + (.971 × Rep. share of two-party **Penn** vote in **2004**)

r^2 .95 (.95 adjusted)   Durbin-Watson score 1.839
t-value 14.697   standard error of the estimate 1.455
(significance .00)

Stark County, Ohio, Equation

Rep. share of two-party **U.S.** vote in **2004** = 7.667 + (.817 × Rep. share of two-party **Stark County** vote in **2004**)

r^2 .95 (.94 adjusted)   Durbin-Watson score 2.077
t-value 14.265   standard error of the estimate 1.497
(significance .00)

Equations are based on data for 13 elections, 1952–2000.
Data Sources: Scammon, McGillivray, and Cook (1997); U.S. Federal Election Commission (2001).

Presidential
Approval Ratings

*If people like the status quo, if they're happy
with what's happening in Washington,
[then Gore will win a Gore-Bush race and]
you can come down and go fishing with
me in Texas.*

George W. Bush
Washington Post
16 June 1999

"Do you approve or disapprove of the way [president's name] is handling his
job as president?" The public's response to this survey question is known as
the presidential approval rating and is an excellent predictor of presidential
election outcomes.

The Gallup Poll has been assessing popular support for the incumbent
president since 1935, and since 1945 has consistently used this wording
(Edwards with Gallup 1990, 3). With the same question, phrased identically in
surveys year after year, it has been possible to make a long-term comparison
of the public's approval of the president and its vote in presidential elections,
thus establishing a link between the two that is useful in election forecasting.

Rationale

The use of presidential approval ratings for forecasting presidential elections
is based on the assumption that voters evaluate the overall performance of a
president, and that this evaluation influences their vote whether to retain the
president's party in the White House—in the person of the incumbent president or other nominee of his party. As Donald J. Devine, an ardent proponent
of this approach to election forecasting, states:

> The theory simply holds that how the public evaluates the performance of
> the political authority in office will determine who will be the next such

officeholder. If the voters believe the incumbent has done well, they will reelect him or vote for his party. If they think he has done poorly, they will vote against him or his party. (Devine 1983, 99)

Early efforts to develop statistical models using presidential approval ratings to forecast presidential elections were limited to elections in which the president was an incumbent running for reelection (Lewis-Beck and Rice 1982; Sigelman 1979). The assumption was that only the president himself would be held accountable for his administration's performance, and that another nominee of this party would not be. In time, however, researchers began including all presidential elections in their analyses, in the belief that the president's *party* is held accountable by voters (Abramowitz 1988, 1996; Brody and Sigelman, 1983; Lewis-Beck and Rice 1992; Lewis-Beck and Tien 1996). Even if the president is not running for reelection personally, the nominee of his party inherits his standing with the public, it is argued, and benefits or suffers accordingly. In short, this approach assumes that presidential elections are *referenda* on the incumbent administration's performance. If so, presidential approval ratings, measures of the administration's standing with the public, can be a useful tool for forecasting presidential elections.

This approach differs from the use of trial heat polls and bellwethers to forecast elections, discussed previously, in that those do not emphasize causes or influences on voting. Apart from a possible bandwagon effect, candidate preference surveys do not cause an election outcome; they reflect whatever factors are influencing the election. The presidential vote in a key bellwether state does not cause the national vote for president; both are responding to whatever common factors are influencing the vote in each setting.

Presidential approval ratings, however, reflect opinion that is **causal**. People may vote for a president or the nominee of that party *because* they believe that the president is doing a good job. Likewise, they may vote against him *because* they believe that he is performing poorly. The public's evaluation of the administration's performance thus is an influence on voting choice and, consequently, on the election outcome.

Establishing the Linkage

In linking presidential approval ratings to election outcomes, I return to the two approaches used in the analysis of trial heats. I first present simple graphic comparisons of approval ratings and election outcomes, attempting to identify the threshold that approval rating scores must cross to result in victory for the incumbent party's candidate. Regression is then used to determine the statistical strength of relationships between ratings and election results, producing more precise forecasts of the percentage vote received by the incumbent party.

In this analysis, as in that of trial heats, I use only presidential approval ratings produced by the Gallup Poll to ensure that the surveys are comparable. There are, however, gaps in Gallup's historical data, as explained by Edwards and Gallup (1990, 3):

Occasional polls did not ask the approval question. It was especially likely to be omitted during presidential election campaigns, when Gallup concluded it could not be asked along with trial-heat questions on presidential candidates because the responses to the trial-heat questions contaminated responses to the approval question and vice versa.

The latest useable dates in which data are available for every election year, beginning in 1952, are in *mid-June*. In 1964, 1972, and 1976 no presidential approval rating surveys were conducted after June—after mid-June in 1976 (Edwards with Gallup 1990, 3, 41, 62, 74). It appears, therefore, that if one uses *individual* Gallup approval ratings in election years, the mid-June surveys are the necessary choice. They are available in each year, and later approval surveys are not.

Some analysts prefer to use *three-month averages* of approval ratings rather than ratings from individual surveys. Averages for the second quarter of election years are favored by political scientists Thomas Holbrook (1996a; 1996b), and Robert Erikson and Christopher Wlezien (1996; Wlezien and Erikson 1996). Another scholar, Douglas Hibbs, has used averages for the election year's third quarter (1982; 1987). Holbrook notes: "Using the average value from this [second quarter] period should help to reduce measurement error that could occur as a result of relying on a single, perhaps aberrant, poll result or relying on polls taken during a single month" (1996b, 508). In essence, Holbrook is concerned that an approval survey conducted at one point in time might not be representative of ratings evident in a more inclusive period. Surveys taken over a wider time span reduce this risk.

Approval indicators both for mid-June and for the second quarter average are used in the following sections to link presidential approval to the incumbent party vote. Data for both indicators are among items reported in Table 3.1.

Graphic Comparison

The results of simple graphic comparisons of presidential approval ratings with election outcomes from 1952 to 2000 are presented in Figures 3.1 and 3.2. As seen in Figure 3.1, for the **mid-June** approval rating, when that rating was 51 percent or higher, the candidate of the incumbent party won, except in 1960, when Nixon lost a close election to Kennedy by 0.2 percent. When the rating was 45 percent or lower, the incumbent party's candidate lost. Thus the **threshold for victory** appears to be **51 percent**, and, on the downside, the **threshold for loss** is **45 percent**. The six percentage points between the two are an inconclusive area. (As in previous chapters, the 2000 election is treated as a "win" for the incumbent party, given that Democrat Gore won the popular vote.)

The **second quarter** average approval ratings produce similar results, evident in Figure 3.2. The lowest winning value from 1952 to 2000 is **49.4 percent** (for 1988), suggesting that as the **win threshold**. The highest losing value is **46.7 percent** (in 1976), thereby becoming the **loss threshold**. A comparison of Figures 3.1 and 3.2 shows that the interval between the win/loss categories for the quarterly average ratings is narrower than for the mid-June ratings, thus providing a less clear demarcation between wins and losses. (The

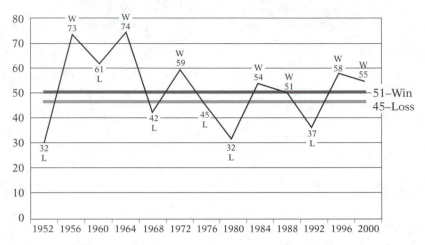

W = Win for candidate of incumbent president's party

L = Loss for candidate of incumbent president's party

1960 is misclassified
2000 is popular vote "win"

Figure 3.1

DATA SOURCES: Edwards with Gallup (1990)
Gallup (various entries listed in Bibliography)

1960 election again was misclassified.) It is clear from the two figures that the outcome of the 1996 election would have been forecast by either the mid-June or average second quarter indicators, using 1952–1992 data. Clinton's ratings for both were well into the victory range. Both figures also would have predicted Gore's close victory in the popular vote in the 2000 election, given Clinton's strong job approval ratings, which were well above the win thresholds.

Regression

Regression equations can be computed in which historical election results are treated as being dependent on presidential approval ratings. This procedure, similar to that in previous chapters, will give us percentage estimates of the vote for the incumbent party's candidate, based on approval ratings.

Using the data presented in Figures 3.1 and 3.2, I have calculated equations derived from approval ratings in mid-June of the election year and from the average ratings in the second quarter. Forecasts of both the 1996 and 2000 elections were generated using this approach. Predictions for 1996 were far superior to those for 2000, primarily because Gore's performance in 2000 failed to match President Clinton's strong job approval ratings. For purposes of illustrating the technique, I thus have chosen the 1996 election. Results for 2000 are reported in Appendix 3.1 at the end of this chapter.

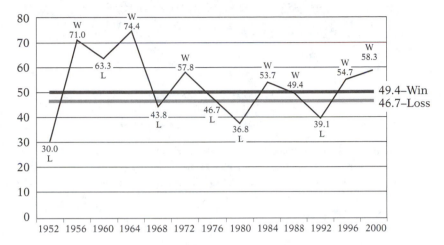

PRESIDENTIAL APPROVAL RATINGS—2ND QUARTER 1952–2000

W = Win for candidate of incumbent president's party

L = Loss for candidate of incumbent president's party

1960 is misclassified
2000 is popular vote "win"

Figure 3.2

DATA SOURCES: Edwards with Gallup (1990)
             Gallup (various entries listed in Bibliography)

Forecasts for 1996 are produced by two equations based on 1952–1992 data; one uses mid-June approval ratings, and the other uses ratings for the second quarter average. The results, reported as equations 3.1 and 3.2, reveal that, of the two, the mid-June equation explains the election outcomes somewhat better. It accounts for 71 percent of the variation in election results, whereas the equation derived from the second quarter ratings accounts for 65 percent.

The historical data for election outcomes and approval ratings for the 1952–1992 period are reported in Table 3.1, as are estimates of the results for each election produced by the regression equation. Also included in the table are the residuals (or errors), numbers that indicate the extent to which estimates of the vote differ from the actual vote for a given election. As evident in the table, the errors vary, ranging from virtually nil to about 7 percent. In both equations, the approval rating correctly indicates the winning candidate in nine elections, but not in two: 1960 and 1976.

Regression Forecasts: 1996

To produce after-the-fact forecasts of the 1996 election outcome, I have substituted the appropriate data from that year into the 1952–1992 equations. The presidential approval rating in mid-June 1996 was 58 percent, as reported by the Gallup Poll (Gallup 1997, 93). That number was entered into the mid-June equation, as follows:

incum. (**Clinton**)
share of two-party = $33.853 + (.368 \times$ Pres. Approval Rating $_{\text{mid-June 1996}})$
vote in **1996**

$\qquad\qquad = 33.853 + (.368 \times 58)$

$\qquad\qquad = \mathbf{55.2\%}$

EQUATION 3.1

r^2 .71 (.67 adjusted)   Durbin-Watson score 1.744
t-value 4.655   standard error of estimate 3.722
   (significance .001)   number of elections 11 (1952–1992)

The resulting forecast of 55.2 percent of the 1996 two-party vote for Clinton is **less than one percent (0.5 percent) in error**, given that Clinton's share of the actual two-party vote was 54.7 percent. The forecast margin of error, however, is large: $+/-$ 8.9 percent with 95 percent probability.

The average second quarter approval rating in 1996 was 54.7 percent (Gallup 1997, 98). This value was entered into that equation with this result:

incum. (**Clinton**)
share of two-party = $33.539 + (.370 \times$ Pres. Approval Rating $_{\text{2nd quarter 1996}})$
vote in **1996**

$\qquad\qquad = 33.539 + (.370 \times 54.7)$

$\qquad\qquad = \mathbf{53.8\%}$

EQUATION 3.2

r^2 .65 (.61 (adjusted)   Durbin-Watson score 2.011
t-value 4.055   standard error of estimate 4.087
   (significance .003)   number of elections 11 (1952–1992)

As for the mid-June forecast for 1996, this forecast based on second quarter approval ratings also is quite accurate, **off only 0.9 percent** from the actual two-party vote for Clinton (54.7 percent). But this model, too, has a large margin of error: $+/-$ 9.7 percent.

Regression Forecasts: Scenarios for 2004

As with other indicators, hypothetical scenarios can be calculated for the impact of presidential approval ratings on election outcomes. Suppose that for the 2004 election one wishes to determine the likely effect on the election of various conceivable presidential approval rating scores in June and in the second quarter. The previous equations (3.1 and 3.2) first need to be recomputed to include data from the most recent elections, 1996 and 2000 in this case. (The updated equations are in Appendix 3.2 at the end of this chapter.) A range of hypothetical approval ratings can be assumed and entered into the two equations. Table 3.2 reports the resulting scenarios. Thus, for example, if one thinks that Bush's approval rating in mid-June 2004 might be 56 percent, the predicted share of the two-party vote for the Republican candidate—presumably Bush running for reelection—would be 54.1 percent. (Using the mid-June equation in Appendix 3.2, the calculations are: $33.873 + [.361 \times 56] = 54.1$.)

Table 3.1 PRESIDENTIAL APPROVAL RATINGS: DATA, REGRESSION ESTIMATES, AND ERRORS: MID-JUNE AND 2ND QUARTER EQUATIONS

Year	(A) Mid-June Pres. Approval	(B) 2nd Qtr. Pres. Appr. (average)	(C) Popular Vote for Incumbent Pres. Party	(D) Estimates of Popular Vote for Eq. 3.1, Mid-June	(E) Error in Mid-June Estimates (C–D)	(F) Estimates of Popular Vote for Eq. 3.2, 2nd Qtr	(G) Error in 2nd qtr. Estimates (C–F)
1952	32	30.0	44.6	45.6	−1.0	44.6	0.0
1956	73	71.0	57.8	60.7	−2.9	59.8	−2.0
1960	61	63.3	49.9	56.3	−6.4	57.0	−7.1
1964	74	74.4	61.3	61.1	0.2	61.1	0.2
1968	42	43.8	49.6	49.3	0.3	49.7	−0.1
1972	59	57.8	61.8	55.5	6.3	54.9	6.9
1976	45	46.7	49.0	50.4	−1.4	50.8	−1.8
1980	32	36.8	44.7	45.6	−0.9	47.2	−2.5
1984	54	53.7	59.2	53.7	5.5	53.4	5.8
1988	51	49.4	53.9	52.6	1.3	51.8	2.1
1992	37	39.1	46.6	47.5	−0.9	48.0	−1.4

All election data are of the two-party vote for the incumbent party candidate.

Data Sources: Edwards with Gallup (1990); Gallup (various entries listed in Bibliography); Scammon and McGillivray (1995).

Table 3.2 SCENARIOS FROM PRESIDENTIAL APPROVAL RATINGS:
VOTE FOR PRESIDENT IN 2004

Bush Approval Rating in 2004	Two-Party Vote for Republican in 2004 Election Based on Approval Ratings (in left column) for Period Indicated Below	
	mid-June	*2nd quarter average*
60%	55.5	55.3
58	54.8	54.6
56	54.1	53.9
54	53.4	53.2
52	52.6	52.5
50	51.9	51.8
48	51.2	51.0
46	50.5	50.3
44	49.8	49.6
42	49.0	48.9
40	48.3	48.2

Example: A second quarter average approval rating for the president of 60 produces a projected election
   result of 55.3 percent of the two-party vote for the Republican candidate.
Results are derived from equations in Appendix 3.2.
Data are for 1952–2000.

Conclusion

In this chapter, the use of presidential approval ratings as an indicator for
forecasting presidential elections has been described. The underlying assumption is that elections are referenda on the performance of the incumbent president, and that voters reward or punish the candidate of the president's party
at the polls accordingly.

In the simplest approach, illustrated in Figures 3.1 and 3.2, approval rating scores for each election were plotted, with victorious elections for the
incumbent party's candidate clustering above an identified threshold, and losing elections falling below a loss threshold. The winner of one election in the
historical data set was wrongly identified. The 1996 and 2000 election outcomes were correctly classified and predicted, at least on a popular vote basis.

In addition, regression equations were computed that linked approval ratings to election results, making percentage forecasts of election outcomes possible. Resulting forecasts for 1996 were close to the actual result, but, as noted
in Appendix 3.1, predictions for the 2000 election indicated that Gore would
fare much better than he did. Clinton's approval ratings were high, but Gore
eked out only a 0.3 percent margin in the two-party popular vote.

Data for approval ratings were for mid-June in one set of calculations and
for the second quarter average in the other. Since these data are available soon
after the surveys are made—early July at the latest—this represents a four-
month forecasting lead time prior to the November election. However, as with
some equations in previous chapters, we encounter large forecast margins of
error in regressions using these indicators.

Appendix 3.1
Forecasts of 2000 Election:
Regressions on Presidential Approval Ratings

Mid-June approval rating

incumbent (**Gore**)
share of two-party = $33.887 + (.366 \times$ Pres. Approval Rating $_{\text{mid-June 2000}})$
vote in **2000**

$= 33.887 + (.366 \times 55)$

$= \textbf{54.0\%}$

r^2 .71 (.68 adjusted)	Durbin-Watson score 1.752
t-value 4.932	standard error of estimate 3.534
(significance .001)	number of elections 12 (1952–1996)

President Clinton's approval rating for mid-June 2000 (55) is inserted into this equation, producing a forecast of 54.0 percent of the two-party vote for Gore (Gallup News Service 2000). This prediction was **3.7 percent in error**, given that Gore in fact received 50.3 percent of the two-party vote. The forecast margin of error is +/− 8.2 percent with 95 percent probability.

Second quarter average rating

incumbent (**Gore**)
share of two-party = $33.545 + (.371 \times$ Pres. Approval Rating $_{\text{2nd quarter 2000}})$
vote in **2000**

$= 33.545 + (.371 \times 58.3)$

$= \textbf{55.2\%}$

r^2 .65 (.61 (adjusted)	Durbin-Watson score 2.030
t-value 4.289	standard error of estimate 3.886
(significance .002)	number of elections 12 (1952–1996)

The average second quarter approval rating for Clinton in 2000 was 58.3 percent (Gallup News Service 2000). Entering this value into the preceding equation produces a forecast of 55.2 percent of the two-party vote for Gore. This **prediction missed** Gore's actual vote share (50.3 percent) by **4.9 percent**. The forecast confidence interval was +/− 9.1 percent.

Data Sources: Scammon, McGillivray, and Cook (1997); Gallup (various entries listed in Bibliography); U.S. Federal Election Commission (2001).

Appendix 3.2
Equations for 2004 Election Scenarios Using Presidential Approval Ratings

Mid-June rating

incumbent (Rep.)
share of two-party $= 33.873 + (.361 \times \text{Pres. Approval Rating}_{\text{mid-June 2004}})$
vote in **2004**

r^2 .68 (.65 adjusted)   Durbin-Watson score 1.702
t-value 4.865   standard error of estimate 3.540
   (significance .001)   number of elections 13 (1952–2000)

Second quarter average rating

incumbent (Rep.)
share of two-party $= 33.925 + (.357 \times \text{Pres. Approval Rating}_{\text{2nd quarter 2004}})$
vote in **2004**

r^2 .60 (.57 adjusted)   Durbin-Watson score 2.043
t-value 4.080   standard error of estimate 3.964
   (significance .002)   number of elections 13 (1952–2000)

Data Sources: Scammon, McGillivray, and Cook (1997); Gallup (various entries listed in Bibliography); U.S. Federal Election Commission (2001).

4
★ ★ ★

Other Public Opinion-Based Techniques

> *On the question of [exit polls'] accuracy, it should be noted in passing that the inveterate political prankster Dick Tuck was able to respond to exit polls in four different states this year by the simple expedient of going into the polling place, asking whether he was registered in that precinct and when the answer was "No," leaving the place to answer exit pollers' questions outside.*

Curtis B. Gans
Executive Director
Committee for the Study of the American Electorate
(in a 1985 Congressional hearing)

As in the preceding chapters, the four approaches discussed here also link public opinion to presidential election forecasts. The first three—exit polls, surveys of respondents' likes and dislikes of candidates, and Pool's "simulmatics" technique—are derived from formal surveys, as are the methods described in previous chapters. The fourth approach, however, differs from these in that the expression of popular opinion about the election is in the context of a stock market environment, in which individuals buy and sell futures on the basis of who they believe will win the election.

Exit Polls

Exit polls are interviews with people as they leave their polling places after having voted, in which they are asked to report their voting choices and to provide information on personal demographics and opinions. Since exit polls' first national use in presidential elections by NBC News in 1980, they have become a regular fixture in election night news coverage.

In presidential elections, exit polls are conducted on a state-by-state basis. Precincts within states are randomly chosen, their chances of being selected depending on the size of their voter pools. By combining results of the state exit polls, a very short range prediction of the national election outcome can be made. The election result thus becomes known a few hours before the actual vote tabulations are completed.

Strictly speaking, exit polls are not true election forecasts because they are conducted while the election is under way, not prior to the balloting. They are not predictions of how people will vote, but rather are estimates as to how people have already voted. In essence, exit polls amount to an acceleration of *reporting* the election outcome. Being contemporaneous with the event, their accuracy is high, although they provide no lead time prior to the election— and only a slight lead prior to the report of the election results.

Exit polls share some of the problems encountered in other face-to-face surveys including high cost and bias that may result from contact between interviewer and respondent. An effort is made to minimize the latter problem by maintaining "voting" anonymity through a procedure in which the person completing the questionnaire does so privately, and places it in a box. Nevertheless, research suggests that bias may persist, such as when the interviewer and interviewee are of different races (Finkel, Guterbock, and Borg 1991).

In a cost containment move, after television networks originally conducted separate exit polls, they joined together to form a survey consortium, which has done their exit polling for presidential elections since 1992. This organization, Voter News Service (originally known as Voter Research and Surveys), makes its poll results available to participating news organizations and does so at the same time for all. Members of Voter News Service include five television networks—ABC, CBS, NBC, Fox, CNN—along with the Associated Press and at least 100 media outlets (Goodfellow 1996).

The most controversial aspect of exit polls relates to the timing of their release. Is it proper for broadcast media to report the results of exit polls before voting places have closed, while people are still voting? On election night in 2000, for example, networks "called" the winner in Florida even though polls were still open in areas of that state in the Central time zone. The problem was compounded when the networks, relying largely on data from exit polls, twice changed their prediction of the victor in Florida.

Disputes over the timing of exit polls' release first became highly contentious following the 1980 election, when it was charged that likely voters in California and other western states failed to vote because the outcome of the presidential election had been established by exit polls conducted in states in time zones further east. State and local races, it was alleged, were thereby impacted, in addition to the states' diminished influence on the national result. As Senator Barbara Boxer of California (then a Representative) said in a Congressional hearing,

> Simply stated, when the networks project winners on election day before some of the polls have closed, would-be voters are discouraged from voting and tend to stay away from the polls. . . . local elections in many states are obviously hindered when would-be voters stay home after learning the national results. More important is the feeling that some voters, particularly in the West, are

irrelevant in Presidential elections. When a citizen in Maine feels their vote counts, but a citizen in California doesn't—simply because of where they live—something is wrong (U.S. House of Representatives 1985, 121).

Beginning in 1981, heavy pressure opposing exit polling was directed against network executives in congressional hearings. Before the 1982 and 1984 elections, Congress passed resolutions requesting that networks make no projections of the election outcome until all polls in the continental United States had closed. Moreover, at least 11 states passed legislation seeking to restrict exit polling. For their part, the networks successfully fought the state laws in court, but agreed not to report the results of a state's exit poll until voting in that state had ended. Networks were steadfast, however, in asserting both the right to report states' exit poll results after polling places in those states had closed and the right to forecast the national election outcome, when that could be done using results of exit polls from those states.

Surveys of Voters' "Likes" and "Dislikes" of Candidates

Rather than asking people directly who they intend to vote for, as in trial heat polls, we may be able to forecast presidential elections by asking them what they like and dislike about the general election candidates. The assumption is that people will vote for a presidential candidate if, on balance, they "like" him more than the other candidate, or at least "dislike" him less. Voters' attitudes toward candidates, therefore, largely determine their voting choice. Proponents of this approach also believe that attitudes toward candidates' political parties can be important, though secondarily.

Princeton's Stanley Kelley, Jr. and Thad Mirer of the University at Albany, SUNY (1974), were early users of this technique, followed by Edward Tufte (1978, 117) and by Kelley (1983) in a later study. Data are derived from the pre-election national surveys, which have been conducted since 1952 by the Institute for Social Research at the University of Michigan. (The first such survey in 1948 occurred after the election.) In extensive interviews respondents are asked questions about a multitude of individual characteristics and attitudes. Among them have been these questions regarding attitudes toward presidential candidates, in wording that has remained virtually identical over the years:

> Now I'd like to ask you about the good and bad points of the two candidates for President. Is there anything in particular about [name of Democratic or Republican candidate] that might make you want to vote for him? What is that? Anything else?
>
> Is there anything in particular about [name of Democratic or Republican candidate] that might make you want to vote against him? What is that? Anything else (Institute for Social Research 1995, questions 401, 402, 405, 406)?

For each person interviewed in this national sample, the number of favorable and unfavorable opinions expressed toward the Democratic candidate is calculated. The same procedure is followed for the Republican. Up to five responses to each "like" and "dislike" question are recorded. Net like/dislike scores are calculated using this procedure:

number of positive mentions of Democrat	*plus*	number of unfavorable mentions of Republican
	MINUS	
number of negative mentions of Democrat	*plus*	number of favorable mentions of Republican

(Institute for Social Research 1995, variable 409; format based on Tufte 1978, 117)

It is assumed that the voter chooses the candidate toward whom he or she has the highest *net* number of favorable mentions. (Kelley [1983, 13] believes that for the voter this process is in fact subconscious.) If there is a tie between the candidates, the voter's party affiliation determines his or her vote. Kelley and Mirer term this concept the Voter's Decision Rule, which they define more specifically as follows:

> The voter canvasses his likes and dislikes of the leading candidates and major parties involved in an election. Weighing each like and dislike equally, he votes for the candidate toward whom he has the greatest net number of favorable attitudes, if there is such a candidate. If no candidate has such an advantage, the voter votes consistently with his party affiliation, if he has one. If his attitudes do not incline him toward one candidate more than toward another, and if he does not identify with one of the major parties, the voter reaches a null decision. . . . Null decisions . . . give us no basis for saying how the voter will vote (Kelley and Mirer 1974, 574).

In a later work, Kelley (1983, 226) reports that for elections from 1952 through 1980, the Voter's Decision Rule correctly predicted the vote of **85.4 percent** of the respondents—an impressive result.

For purposes of election forecasting, the greatest shortcoming of this approach is that the American National Election Studies (ANES) pre-election surveys on which it is based are *not released until **after** the election*—a limitation underscored in Rice (1985), Erikson (1989a), and Norpoth (1996). Thus, the Kelley model and others based on these ANES data (e.g., Tufte 1978) have no apparent usefulness in making pre-election forecasts. However, this technique, reliable and proven, is available for organizations that have the resources to implement it, such as commercial polling firms, which could add the like/dislike questions to other pre-election surveys. With results thereby available before the election, forecasts of the outcome using this technique could then be produced.

Surveys of Past and Present Demographics: Ithiel de Sola Pool's "Simulmatics"

The forecasting techniques considered thus far have linked voters' opinions to election outcomes, when the opinion surveys occur in the contemporaneous election cycle. By contrast, Ithiel de Sola Pool, the late MIT political communications pioneer, and colleagues developed a forecasting approach in which the point of departure was surveys made at the time of the *previous election*. They dubbed this technique "simulmatics." In analyzing those prior surveys, Pool's team attempted to determine the issue positions and voting patterns of people with similar demographic characteristics. During the next election cycle, they used *current* surveys to determine the proportion of voters then in the respective demographic categories identified earlier. They assumed that people with similar demographic characteristics would continue to vote in the present as they had in the past. If so, forecasts of the current election outcome could be generated by determining the number of voters in the respective demographic categories and summing across the categories for a grand total (Pool, Abelson, and Popkin 1965; Armstrong 1985, 70–71).

For example, suppose that a demographic group, constituting 10 percent of the electorate, is comprised of older Catholic women of modest means living in cities in the northeastern part of the country. Further assume that surveys made at the time of the previous election determined that individuals with these characteristics tended to be pro-labor and in favor of social spending programs, and that 80 percent of them voted Democratic in presidential elections. With this group being 10 percent of the electorate and voting 80 percent Democratic, this means that they accounted for 8 percent of the electorate voting Democratic and 2 percent of the electorate voting Republican (.10 × .80, and .10 × .20, respectively). Now suppose that four years later women with these characteristics constitute 15 percent of the electorate, rather than the previous 10 percent. If their past voting patterns hold at 80 percent Democratic, we would expect 12 percent of the electorate, represented by this group, to vote Democratic and 3 percent to vote Republican in the current election (.15 × .80, and .15 × .20, respectively).

As noted, we are assuming that most people with the characteristics described vote Democratic. But what about an older woman of modest means living in a northeastern city who is *Protestant*? Being Protestant, yet having the other characteristics, does not fit the usual pattern. Such voters are subject to what Pool terms "cross-pressures." Because they are urban, in the northeast, elderly, female, and of modest means, they would be expected to vote Democratic. But they are also Protestants, and most Protestants vote Republican. Thus a Protestant with these other pro-Democratic characteristics would be a less dependable Democratic voter than if she were Catholic.

The approach that Pool took to deal with cross-pressured voters was to ascertain relevant attitudes of persons with these characteristics, as evident in surveys made at the time of the mid-term Congressional elections two years previously. Specifically, did those surveys reveal anti-Catholic bias among those voters? If so, they were omitted from the percent voting Democratic in the current presidential election. For example, if this cross-pressured group comprised 5 percent of the current electorate and in previous elections 60 percent had voted Democratic, that group would constitute 3 percent of the electorate's support for the Democrat (.05 × .60). Suppose that current surveys show that 50 percent of this group has anti-Catholic bias. Pool would reduce the expected Democratic vote from this group by 50 percent, down to 30 percent of the group, which is 1.5 percent of the total electorate (.05 × .30).

Pool's simulmatics technique was initially applied in the 1960 presidential campaign to assist the Democratic campaign organization, primarily in developing strategies for dealing with issues such as Kennedy's Catholicism. Four years later, the technique was also used by the Johnson campaign.

Pool's 1960 work with surveys began with a myriad of voter and issue cells, which reduced to 480 categories, crossing respondents' issue positions with demographic characteristics. This was a monumental effort, particularly for that time, processing surveys and computing results for all of the categories. The technique was cumbersome and expensive to implement. Though not known to be in current use, it is noteworthy as a pioneering early election forecasting method, making unique use of survey research.

Iowa Electronic Market

I now turn to a method of forecasting presidential elections that, like those discussed previously, is based on public opinion, but with novel differences: First, the public's views are expressed in a stock market environment rather than in surveys. Second, it is a limited public, comprised of market traders. Third, by their actions, the market traders are expressing their views as to who they believe will win rather than who they personally want to win.

The Iowa Electronic Market is the brainchild of members of the business faculty at the University of Iowa (Berg et al. 1997a; Berg et al. 1997b; Forsythe et al. 1994; Forsythe et al. 1992). It began as the Iowa Political Stock Market in 1988 and has functioned in the succeeding presidential elections as well. In this market, traders buy and sell futures contracts representing the candidates in an upcoming election. The value of a contract at a given time depends on market forces, in that sense representing the composite view of traders as to that candidate's chances of winning the election. In practice, the market has been a highly accurate predictor of presidential elections.

In one format—the *vote-share* market—traders estimate the percentage of the popular vote likely to be received by a candidate and make trades accordingly. For example, suppose that at one point in the 1992 campaign Bush contracts were selling for 40 cents. That means that the market consensus was that Bush would receive 40 percent of the vote; when the election was over, Bush contracts would be liquidated at that price if his vote share was 40 percent. If a trader bought 100 shares of Bush at 40 cents (for $40) and the market consensus of Bush's chances improved so that a month later Bush contracts were selling for 45 cents, the trader could sell the 100 shares for a $5 gain on the transaction. Conversely, the trader's shares would be worth less than he paid if the later market consensus was that Bush would receive less than 40 percent of the vote.

Another version of the market in presidential election futures also has existed. In this one, the *"winner takes all"* in that when the election is over all contracts for the winning candidate are liquidated at $1.00 per share. All contracts for any other candidate become worthless. Suppose that in 1996 a trader bought 100 Clinton shares at 50 cents (for $50). After Clinton won the election, when contracts were settled, the trader would receive $1.00 for each

Clinton share, thus $100. Those who owned shares of the Republican challenger, Dole, would receive nothing. Of course, traders can get out of the market at any time before the election, selling their shares at current value rather than holding them until liquidation.

Anyone can become a trader in this market by opening an account for as little as $5 or as much as $500. There are no commissions on trades, which are all handled on-line by computers housed at the University of Iowa. Not surprisingly, most participants are university students and faculty members. Participation details are available on the market's Web site (**www.biz.uiowa. edu/iem/markets**). Other markets have been created, trading futures on which party will control the House and Senate after Congressional elections. Markets have even been set up for elections in other countries.

The Iowa Electronic Market successfully forecast the 1988, 1992, and 1996 presidential elections, the final pre-election value of contracts in the vote-share market being very close to the election outcomes. In 2000, the percent difference between the major candidates in the vote share market was close throughout the entire market period beginning in January. This is evident in Figure 4.1, which tracks the values of vote share contracts as priced on the left vertical scale. On the day before this election, November 6, trading in the Bush contract closed at $.520, meaning that traders thought that Bush would

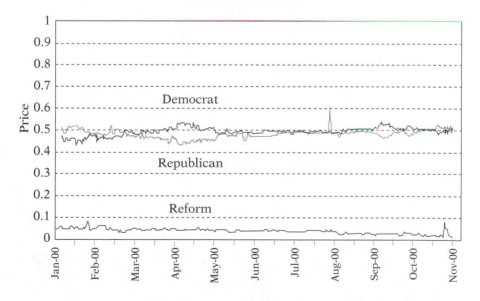

IOWA ELECTRONIC MARKET 2000 PRESIDENTIAL ELECTION: VOTE-SHARE MARKET

Figure 4.1

SOURCE: Iowa Electronic Market Web site (**www.biz.uiowa.edu/iem**)

receive 52.0 percent of the vote. The Gore contract was valued at $.475 and the Reform candidate Buchanan's at $.017. (Contracts for Green Party candidate Ralph Nader were not offered.) Thus, at that point in the market, the election outcome was expected to be 4.5 percent in Bush's favor over Gore (52.0 percent minus 47.5 percent). By contrast, two days before the election, November 5, the market lead had been reversed, with Gore ahead of Bush by 1.3 percent. The electronic market thus seemed to capture the volatility within the electorate during the last days of the 2000 campaign, while in the end failing to predict Gore's close win in the popular vote. No doubt traders were influenced to some extent by final surveys of the major trial heat polls, which were near unanimous in predicting a Bush victory.

Apart from the market result in 2000, why has this approach been successful in forecasting presidential elections? The argument is that traders are effective processors of information that they glean from a variety of sources. They are motivated by their own money being at risk and thus may act in a more thoughtful manner than, say, someone responding to a survey. Perhaps traders do not even have to be very well informed for the system to work well. The originators of the project contend that it supports the Hayek hypothesis, "which asserts that markets can work correctly even if the participants have very limited knowledge about their environment or about other participants" (Forsythe et al. 1992, 1143).

5

★ ★ ★

Judgment-Based Forecasting Techniques

. . . [In the fall of 1948] Newsweek magazine was taking a poll of fifty highly regarded political writers. . . . . Of the writers polled, not one thought Truman would win. The vote was unanimous, 50 for Dewey, 0 for Truman . . . [When he saw the magazine Truman said]
"I know every one of these 50 fellows. There isn't one of them has enough sense to pound sand in a rat hole."

David McCullough
Truman (1992)
[emphasis added]

Most of the techniques for forecasting presidential elections described in this book are based on data gathered and analyzed in a manner that minimizes the researcher's opinions. Following in the tradition of science, analysts are presumed to be dispassionate observers who seek to neutralize their own views. In this chapter, however, I present forecasting techniques in which expert judgment and informed opinions are explicitly factored into the forecasting process.

First, I describe an approach in which two researchers have rated the strengths and liabilities of both major political parties in a series of presidential elections, producing scores of net party strength, which they then relate to election results through regression. This method thus blends the analysts' judgment with statistics. Second, I review a technique in which one scholar has identified 13 factors believed to impact presidential election outcomes. The incumbent party is forecast to either win or lose, depending on whether the required number of indicators is judged to be in that party's favor. Third, I consider two techniques in which experts comprising a panel are surveyed for their estimates of future election outcomes, the forecast being the group's composite view. In the final section, I illustrate the means by which expected utility theory can be applied to forecasting presidential elections. Expected utility theory and expert panels have been little used for predicting U.S. presidential elections, but these techniques have a record of other successful applications and appear to have promise in election forecasting.

Judgment-Based Regression: Budge and Farlie

Two British scholars, Ian Budge and Dennis J. Farlie, have developed an approach to forecasting elections that is a blend of expert opinion and the regression statistical method. We have seen in previous chapters how regression has been used to relate public opinion, expressed in trial heat polls and presidential approval ratings, to election outcomes. In their approach, Budge and Farlie make judgments of party strength and weakness, reduce those judgments to quantitative scores, and then link the scores to election results with regression. Their method is not intended to be unique to U.S. elections, and, in fact, has been applied to 23 stable democracies (Budge and Farlie 1983).

Underlying this approach is the assumption that in elections voters' concerns may relate to any of 14 key issue areas, which are listed in Table 5.1. Observing the campaign and mood of the electorate in a given election, the analyst first determines what issues, if any, in each of the 14 categories are important to voters. A salience score is then assigned to each identified issue, which represents the issue's potential impact on the election outcome:

0 = no impact
1 = small impact
2 = medium impact
3 = large impact

The analyst next determines which party is affected by the issue and whether that impact is positive or negative for the party.

As an example, let us look at issue scores compiled by Budge and Farlie for the 1972 election, which are summarized in Table 5.2. This election effectively illustrates the way that scores are assigned and tallied across several categories; some are positive and some are negative for the candidates. In 1972, issues in six of 14 categories were judged to be important, with two helpful to the Republican, Nixon; one helpful to the Democrat, McGovern; and three harmful to McGovern. None of these issues was seen as negative for Nixon. As evident in the table, the net issue scores were +6 for Nixon and −3 for McGovern.

Using this approach, Budge and Farlie calculated issue scores for the Democratic and Republican presidential candidates in elections from 1948 through 1980. (These results are shown in Table 5.3.) They then regressed each

Table 5.1 BUDGE AND FARLIE: POTENTIAL ISSUES THAT VOTERS CONSIDER

Broad Grouping	Specific Campaign Issues Within Each Broad Grouping
1. Civil order	Law and order; measures against crime; death penalty; rioting, strikes and demonstrations; anti-system parties and problems caused by their strength.
2. Constitutional	Questions involving established institutions (e.g., monarchy, presidency, parliament and relations between them); democracy; civil rights.
3. Foreign relationships	Membership of NATO and other foreign alliances; detente; attitude to Communist powers; entry to EEC; national prestige abroad; colonies and decolonization, overseas aid; attitudes to war and peace (Vietnam).
4. Defense	Military spending increases, reduction, importance vis-a-vis other policy areas; nuclear arms.
5. Candidate reactions and prospects	Likes and dislikes about candidates; leading candidates' performance.
6. Government record	Current financial situation and prospects, expectations; economic prosperity, depression. Incidence of inflation and unemployment; government corruption, inefficiency; satisfaction with government in general and in any specified area in ways not stipulated in other categories. Is tax money spent wisely? Desire for majority government, strong government.
7. Moral-religious	Support of traditional/Christian morals and church; abortion and birth control; temperance; anti-clericalism–danger from clergy/church; religious schools and education.
8. Ethnic	Immigration and foreign workers; attitudes to minority groups and their advancement; discrimination; school and housing integration; language questions.
9. Regional	National unity; devolution and regional autonomy; regional equalization of resources.

(continued)

Table 5.1 (CONTINUED)

Broad Grouping	Specific Campaign Issues Within Each Broad Grouping
10. Urban-rural	Farmers and rural interests; agricultural subsidies.
11. Socioeconomic redistribution	Social service spending; importance of social welfare; housing as a problem; housing subsidies; rent control; food subsidies; health and medical services; social reform; pensions; aid to other services such as education; action in regard to unemployment; full employment, employment guarantee.
12. Government control and planning	Nationalization; state control of the economy; general government power and control; management and regulation of environment.
13. Government regulation in favor of the individual	Action against monopolies; big business power; trade union power; protectionism and free trade.
14. Initiative and freedom	Closed shop and action in relation to it; incentives; level of taxation; support for free enterprise economics.

Source: Ian Budge and Dennis J. Farlie, *Explaining and Predicting Elections: Issue Effects and Party Strategies in Twenty-Three Democracies* (London: George Allen and Unwin, 1983), pp. 28–30. Copyright 1983 by Ian Budge and Dennis J. Farlie. Reprinted by permission.

party's percentage of the popular vote on that party's issue scores, producing these two equations (1983, 69, 72, 82):

Dem. Pres. candidate
% of total **vote**   =   48.2 + (2.08 × net **Dem. issue score**)

EQUATION 5.1

Rep. Pres. candidate
% of total **vote**   =   48.1 + (1.31 × net **Rep. issue score**)

EQUATION 5.2

The constant in each regression, 48.2 for the Democrats and 48.1 for the Republicans, is the vote that each party would receive if issues had no impact on that party's candidate in an election. (Mathematically, an issue score of zero, multiplied by the slope [2.08 for the Democrat or 1.31 for the Republican], leaves only the constant.) This represents the "recurring level of support" for the party, the apparent impact of party identification on the vote (1983, 73). Budge and Farlie term this the "Basic Vote," which, interestingly, is virtually identical for both Democrats and Republicans.

Table 5.2 BUDGE AND FARLIE: CALCULATION OF ISSUE SCORES
TO FORECAST 1972 ELECTION

Issue Description	Issue Category	Issue Score	Party Impacted
Vietnam peace negotiations	3	+3	Rep.
Prestige of sitting president	5	+3	Rep.
net score for **Republican +6**			Rep.
Lack of credibility of Democrat: Eagleton affair	6	−3	Dem.
McGovern's projected cuts in defense expenditures	4	−2	Dem.
McGovern's advocacy of "big government"	14	−1	Dem.
Proposal for payments to poor by federal government	11	+3	Dem.
net score for **Democrat −3**			Dem.

Source: Adapted from Ian Budge and Dennis J. Farlie, *Explaining and Predicting Elections: Issue Effects and Party Strategies in Twenty-Three Democracies* (London: George Allen and Unwin, 1983), p. 211. Copyright 1983 by Ian Budge and Dennis J. Farlie. Reprinted by permission.

Table 5.3 BUDGE AND FARLIE:
ISSUE SCORES AND VOTE RECEIVED BY PRESIDENTIAL CANDIDATES, 1948–1980

Year	Rep. Issue Score	Rep. % of Total Vote	Dem. Issue Score	Dem. % of Total Vote
1948	−1	45.1	1	49.6
1952	6	55.1	−4	44.4
1956	9	57.4	0	42.0
1960	0	49.5	0	49.7
1964	−6	38.5	6	61.1
1968	1	43.4	−1	42.7
1972	6	60.7	−3	37.5
1976	0	48.0	0	50.1
1980	1	51.0	−1	41.0

Source: Ian Budge and Dennis J. Farlie, *Explaining and Predicting Elections: Issue Effects and Party Strategies in Twenty-Three Democracies* (London: George Allen and Unwin, 1983), p. 173. [Party headings changed slightly.] Copyright 1983 by Ian Budge and Dennis J. Farlie. Reprinted by permission.

To obtain a forecast for a party's candidate in an upcoming presidential election, the analyst calculates the party's scores on individual issues relevant to that election and sums them for an overall net score, as described previously. This net score is then inserted into that party's regression equation to produce a forecast of the party's percentage of the vote. Returning to the 1972 election, I obtained this percentage forecast for Nixon, using equation 5.2 and data from Table 5.2:

> Republican **(Nixon)**
> share of total vote in 1972 $\;= \;48.1 + (1.31 \times \mathbf{6})$
> $\qquad\qquad\qquad\qquad\;\;\; = \;48.1 + 7.86$
> $\qquad\qquad\qquad\qquad\;\;\; = \;\mathbf{56.0\%}$

Nixon, in fact, received **60.7 percent** of the vote, a forecast error of 4.7 percent. (Budge and Farlie use candidate shares of the total vote, not shares of the two-party vote that I have used elsewhere.)

The predicted vote for Nixon's opponent, McGovern, can be calculated as follows from equation 5.1, again with data from Table 5.2:

> Democrat **(McGovern)**
> share of total vote in 1972 $\;= 48.2 + (2.08 \times \mathbf{-3})$
> $\qquad\qquad\qquad\qquad\;\;\; = 48.1 + (-6.24)$
> $\qquad\qquad\qquad\qquad\;\;\; = \mathbf{41.9\%}$

McGovern's share of the total vote was **37.5 percent**, which is 4.4 percent lower than the forecast.

Assessments of Key Factors Affecting Elections: Lichtman

In 1981, historian Allan Lichtman of American University developed a technique for forecasting presidential elections, which, as in the Budge and Farlie approach, is based on the author's evaluation of conditions pertinent to the election. Thus, Lichtman does not predict election outcomes directly, but makes judgments of the current status of specific factors thought to influence the result of any presidential election. In a given election, these 13 "keys" are determined to be operating either in favor of the incumbent party's candidate or against him. If the number of keys working against the incumbent crosses a given threshold, that candidate is then forecast to lose the election. Otherwise, the incumbent wins.

As seen in Table 5.4, Lichtman's 13 keys cover a wide range of possible influences on an election, including economic conditions, social unrest, administration policies, candidate characteristics, and the like. The keys are declarative statements that are worded in such a way that, if true, they work to the advantage of the incumbent party's candidate. Conversely, if they are false, the challenger benefits.

Since each indicator statement is judged to be either true or false, the analyst must weigh the evidence, and often there are facts supporting the statement and facts contradicting the statement. Thus, one must decide whether, *on balance*, the statement is true or false. Once it is determined whether the weight of the evidence causes the indicator to cross the threshold, or not, the number of false statements is counted. Lichtman has determined historically that if five or fewer of the statements in Table 5.4 are false, the incumbent party's candidate will likely win. If six or more statements are false, the incum-

Table 5.4 LICHTMAN'S 13 KEYS TO THE WHITE HOUSE

The Keys to the White House are stated as conditions that favor reelection of the incumbent party. When five or fewer statements are false, the incumbent party wins. When six or more are false, the incumbent party loses.

KEY 1   **Incumbent party mandate:** After the mid-term elections, the incumbent party holds more seats in the U.S. House of Representatives than it did after the previous mid-term elections.

KEY 2   **Nomination-contest:** There is no serious contest for the incumbent party nomination.

KEY 3   **Incumbency:** The incumbent party candidate is the sitting president.

KEY 4   **Third party:** There is no significant third-party or independent campaign.

KEY 5   **Short-term economy:** The economy is not in recession during the election campaign.

KEY 6   **Long-term economy:** Real annual per-capita economic growth during the term equals or exceeds mean growth during the two previous terms.

KEY 7   **Policy change:** The incumbent administration effects major changes in national policy.

KEY 8   **Social unrest:** There is no sustained social unrest during the term.

KEY 9   **Scandal:** The incumbent administration is untainted by major scandal.

KEY 10 **Foreign or military failure:** The incumbent administration suffers no major failure in foreign or military affairs.

KEY 11 **Foreign or military success:** The incumbent administration achieves a major success in foreign or military affairs.

KEY 12 **Incumbent charisma:** The incumbent party candidate is charismatic or a national hero.

KEY 13 **Challenger charisma:** The challenging party candidate is not charismatic or a national hero.

Source: Allan J. Lichtman, *The Keys to the White House, 1996: A Surefire Guide to Predicting the Next President* (Lanham, MD: Madison Books, 1996), p. 3. Copyright 1996 by Madison Books, Inc. Reprinted by permission.

bent will lose and the challenger will win. (Stated positively, if eight or more of the statements are true, the incumbent party candidate will win. If only seven or fewer are true, the incumbent will lose.) This rule determines the predicted outcome for an upcoming election.

As a review of Table 5.4 reveals, all but one of the keys are unrelated to the challenger candidate. (The exception is Key 13, challenger charisma.) In this scheme, the quality of the challenger's campaign has no bearing on the election outcome. Rather, the election is largely a referendum on the incumbent administration, its performance in office and occurrences in the political and economic environment during that time. This assumption is similar to the rationale of forecasts based on presidential approval ratings discussed in Chapter 3.

The subjective nature of most of the indicator statements is also apparent. Different analysts might interpret words in the statements and relevant events differently. For example, what is a *major* success in foreign or military affairs (Key 11), a *significant* third-party or independent campaign (Key 4), or *sustained* social unrest (Key 8)? Consider Lichtman's analysis of Key 9 for the 1980 election, regarding major administration scandal, in which the weight of the evidence seems less than obvious (and which Lichtman concedes was a difficult call):

> He [Carter] had been embarrassed by a succession of incidents: the resignation of his longtime friend, budget director Bert Lance, over the disclosure of irregularities in the conduct of his banking business; allegations of cocaine use and other unseemly behavior by his chief of staff, Hamilton Jordan; and revelations during the campaign that the president's brother Billy had become a paid agent of the government of Libya—the so-called "Billygate" affair. But even the cumulative impact of these incidents did not compare to such historical precedents as the Teapot Dome scandals of the Harding administration, the "mess in Washington" of the Truman years, or the Watergate break-in and subsequent cover-up by the Nixon administration, so Key 9 stayed in the Democrats' column (Lichtman and DeCell 1990, 22).

The patterns that Lichtman initially identified are found in the elections from 1860 through 1980. His indicator statements were developed and refined to classify these elections as wins or losses for the incumbent, as he reported in Table 5.5. With a system in place, based on these historical data, Lichtman has made forecasts for the elections of 1984, 1988, 1992, 1996, and 2000. As evident in Table 5.5, each of these forecasts has accurately predicted the winner of the popular vote. In 1996, Lichtman published a book that predicted Clinton's reelection, 10 months before the election: "Barring an economic reversal, a humiliation abroad, or dramatic Whitewater developments, he [Clinton] will almost certainly be reelected president, no matter what third-party contenders decide to do in 1996" (1996a, 182).

As he looked toward the 2000 election, Lichtman published a preliminary analysis in November 1999, concluding that the direction of 12 of the 13 keys could tentatively be determined at that time, a year ahead. He found the statements in Keys 1, 4, 5, 6, 8, 10, and 13 to all be true, therefore favoring the incumbent Democratic party's candidate. The five statements comprising Keys 3, 7, 9, 11, and 12 were false and thus negative for the Democrat. The result for Key 2 was found to be uncertain. According to Lichtman's decision rule, the Democratic candidate would win if five of the key statements were false, but would lose if six were false. The outcome for Key 2 thus became critical.

The statement comprising Key 2 declares: "There is no serious contest for the incumbent party nomination." The emergence of a serious contest for the Democratic nomination in 2000 would have added a crucial sixth negative key for the Democratic candidate, crossing the threshold from victory to defeat. What is a "serious" contest for the Democratic nomination? Lichtman gives a precise answer: It is one in which the Democratic nominee fails to control at least two-thirds of the delegates to the national convention and fails to win the nomination on the first ballot (1999, 424). At the time of Lichtman's writing,

Table 5.5 LICHTMAN: APPLICATION OF 13 KEYS TO ELECTIONS, 1860–2000

Key #	1	2	3	4	5	6	7	8	9	10	11	12	13	Total False (Xs)
Incumbent Victories														
1864	O	O	O	O	O	X	O	X	O	O	O	X	O	3
1868	O	O	X	O	O	O	O	X	O	O	O	O	O	2
1872	X	O	O	O	O	O	X	X	O	O	O	O	O	3
1880	O	X	X	O	O	O	O	O	O	O	X	X	O	4
1888	X	O	O	O	O	O	X	X	O	O	X	X	O	5*
1900	X	O	O	O	O	O	O	O	O	O	O	X	X	3
1904	O	O	O	O	O	O	O	O	O	O	O	O	O	0
1908	O	O	X	O	O	X	O	O	O	O	O	X	O	3
1916	X	O	O	O	O	X	O	O	O	O	O	X	O	3
1924	X	O	O	X	O	O	O	O	X	O	O	X	O	4
1928	O	O	X	O	O	O	X	O	O	O	O	X	O	3
1936	O	O	O	O	O	O	O	O	O	O	X	O	O	1
1940	X	O	O	O	O	O	O	O	O	O	X	O	O	2
1944	X	O	O	O	O	O	O	O	O	X	O	O	O	2
1948	X	O	O	X	O	X	O	O	O	X	O	X	O	5
1956	O	O	O	O	O	O	X	O	O	O	O	O	O	1
1964	X	O	O	O	O	O	O	O	O	X	O	X	O	3
1972	X	O	O	O	O	X	X	O	O	O	O	X	O	4
1984	O	O	O	O	O	X	O	O	O	O	X	O	O	2
1988	O	O	X	O	O	O	X	O	O	O	O	X	O	3
1996	X	O	O	X	O	O	X	O	O	O	X	X	O	5
2000	O	O	X	O	O	O	X	O	X	O	X	X	O	5*
Challenger Victories														
1860	O	X	X	X	O	O	X	X	O	O	X	X	O	7
1876	X	X	X	O	X	X	X	O	X	O	X	X	O	9*
1884	X	X	X	O	X	X	X	O	O	O	X	O	O	7
1892	X	X	O	X	O	O	O	X	O	O	X	X	O	6
1896	X	X	O	X	X	X	X	X	O	O	X	O	O	8
1912	X	X	O	X	O	O	X	O	O	O	X	X	O	6
1920	X	X	O	X	X	X	O	X	O	X	O	X	O	8
1932	X	O	O	O	X	X	X	X	O	O	X	X	X	8
1952	O	X	X	O	O	X	X	O	X	X	O	X	X	8
1960	X	O	X	O	X	X	X	O	O	X	X	X	X	9
1968	X	X	X	X	O	O	O	X	O	X	X	X	O	8
1976	X	X	O	O	O	X	X	O	X	X	X	X	O	8
1980	X	X	O	X	X	O	X	O	O	X	O	X	X	8
1992	X	O	O	X	X	X	X	O	O	O	X	O	O	6

1. Party mandate
2. Nomination contest
3. Incumbency
4. Third party
5. Short-term economy
6. Long-term economy
7. Policy change
8. Social unrest
9. Scandal
10. Foreign/military failure
11. Foreign/military success
12. Incumbent charisma
13. Challenger charisma

X = false
O = true

*Electoral vote did not coincide with popular vote results.

Source: Allan J. Lichtman, *The Keys to the White House, 1996: A Surefire Guide to Predicting the Next President* (Lanham, MD: Madison Books, 1996), p. 21. Copyright 1996 by Madison Books, Inc. Reprinted by permission. Data for 1996 are from Lichtman (1996a) and personal communication from the author. Data for 2000 are from Lichtman (1999).

it was unclear whether the spirited Democratic competition between former Senator Bill Bradley and Vice President Al Gore would deny the eventual nominee two-thirds of the delegates and a first ballot nomination. Lichtman wrote: ". . . Democrats will win in 2000 if, and only if, they unite around a single presidential candidate" (1999, 424). Of course, in time the Democrats did unite around a single candidate, as Gore cruised to an easy nomination after Bradley's withdrawal in March.

With Key 2 in the Democrats' favor, Lichtman's original analysis, dating from a year before the election, could then be extended to predict a victory for Gore. This forecast was accurate, for the Lichtman approach is designed to predict the winner of the *popular* vote. Thus, as noted in Table 5.5, the elections of 1876 and 1888 also are classified as victories for the popular vote winners— Tilden and Cleveland, respectively—despite their losses in the Electoral College.

Panels of Experts

In this section, two related methods are described that derive forecasts from surveys of panels of experts formed by the analyst. Each forecast is a representation of the collective judgment of experts in the group.

Mid-Point of Experts' Collective Opinions

This approach is the essence of simplicity. The analyst identifies knowledgeable experts, secures their participation, and then surveys the group members as to their estimates of probable outcomes. The forecast is either the average or mid-point of the collective opinions.

Point forecasts are possible using this approach. As applied to elections, each expert can be asked to predict the share of the vote likely to be received by the Democrat, Republican, and significant minor candidates. These estimates are then averaged, or the median (middle) score is determined. Alternatively, the experts can merely be asked for their predictions of the winner, with the forecast being the candidate seen as the likely winner by the majority on the panel.

One example in which this technique could easily have been applied is the expert survey conducted by *Washington Post* columnist David Broder a few days before the 1992 election (Broder 1992). Broder's group was comprised primarily of Washington-based journalists and politicos, 15 in all. Though Broder did not summarize the individuals' predictions—only reporting them separately— I calculated the average forecast for the group to be 45.7 percent for Clinton, 40.6 percent for Bush, and 12.9 percent for Perot. (The total does not add to 100 percent because of vote shares allocated to other candidates.) The election outcome was 43.0 percent, 37.4 percent, and 19.5 percent for the candidates, respectively, resulting in a forecast error of 2.7 percent for Clinton, 3.2 percent for Bush, and 6.6 percent for Perot. If we consider only results for candidates of the two major parties, the collective forecast of the group was much better. Clinton was predicted to receive 53.0 percent of the two-party vote and in fact garnered 53.5 percent. Thus Broder's panel was off by only 0.5 percent.

Apart from the Broder example, it is difficult to identify published applications of this approach to presidential election forecasting. The technique of polling experts for their composite opinion, however, has been used for years in forecasting economic conditions and corporate earnings. The authoritative monthly newsletter, *Blue Chip Economic Indicators*, regularly surveys its panel of 50 prominent economists and publishes their average estimate of future U.S. economic growth. *Consensus Economics* tracks economists' predictions of growth internationally. *First Call* surveys securities analysts, publishing their consensus estimates of corporate earnings. These collective forecasts in economics and business have been reasonably accurate. In fact, the accuracy of growth forecasts from the *Blue Chip* consensus usually rivals that from large econometric models.

Despite few election applications thus far, this approach could be usefully adapted to forecasting presidential elections. A panel of experts—journalists, academics, scholars in research organizations—could be surveyed regularly for their assessments of prospective candidates' strength during the presidential primaries and, as the campaign progresses, surveyed for their forecasts of the election outcome.

Delphi Surveys

The Delphi technique, developed in the 1950s at the Rand Corporation, is a variant to the approach of generating forecasts by surveying panels of experts (Linstone and Turoff 1975; Rowe, Wright, and Bolger 1991; Rowe and Wright 1999). It, too, is little used in presidential election forecasting, but easily could be applied to this purpose.

In the Delphi approach, greater care is given to method and procedure than merely using the mid-point of experts' forecasts. Delphi surveys share these essential characteristics: First, members of the panel who complete written questionnaires are anonymous to one another. This is done so that individual participants will feel no social pressure from within the group to adopt a particular viewpoint, but rather will be guided only by their best judgment. Second, members of the panel are provided with summaries of the answers of other panelists, often the group's mean (average) or median responses for quantitative answers. Panelists are then asked to review their own initial responses and given an opportunity to change them in light of the group's collective opinion. Anonymity is important so that members can change their responses, if they believe appropriate, without loss of face for doing so. This process of feedback and adjustment may continue for multiple rounds until a consensus emerges. The final result normally is the mean or median of panelists' responses in the final round, with all members' views being weighted equally (Rowe and Wright 1999, 354). Obviously, the Delphi technique promotes consensus among the panelists in that those who make extreme initial forecasts are encouraged to reevaluate their estimates in light of the group's projections. It is assumed, therefore, that the group consensus is more likely to be accurate than any individual's estimate, especially someone with an extreme position.

Delphi has been commonly used in predicting responses to defense strategies and in forecasting trends in science and technology, health care, marketing, and education. This technique could easily be applied to forecasting presidential elections by enlisting knowledgeable journalists, academics, and politicos who might participate, even some who might otherwise be reluctant to do so were anonymity not provided. Successive rounds of responses could continue throughout the election season.

Expected Utility Theory

I now turn to expected utility theory, the application of which to politics has been pioneered by Bruce Bueno de Mesquita of the Hoover Institution at Stanford University. The fundamental assumption is that people act in a rational manner, choosing alternatives that they expect will benefit them most. By identifying these alternatives for key players in a political process and determining the players' influence, analysts can thereby forecast the outcome. This approach has been applied to forecasting such phenomena as regime change, government policies, the political future of Hong Kong under Chinese rule, and the likelihood of war. Many of the theory's forecasting applications have been made within, or for, the Central Intelligence agency and are classified. In fact, an agency official reported that from 1982 to 1991 expected utility models were used there "to analyze and identify policy choice scenarios for over 1,000 issues in scores of countries" with more than 90 percent accuracy (Bueno de Mesquita 1997, 260).

Despite numerous applications, however, expected utility theory has been used only occasionally for election forecasting. Apparently, just four elections have been publicly reported as being forecast by this technique: the 1985 presidential election in Brazil (Feder 1995, 284), the 1990 elections in Nicaragua (Ray and Russett 1996, 449), the 1992 French referendum on acceptance of the European Union's Maastricht Treaty (Organski and Bueno de Mesquita 1993), and the 1996 Russian presidential election (Abdollahian and Kugler 1997, 276–278). A forecast of the 1996 U.S. presidential election using expected utility theory was made by the late University of Michigan political scientist, A. F. K. Organski, but is unpublished (Organski 1997). Given the successful record in forecasting other phenomena, this technique has considerable potential for expanded application to election forecasting, including U.S. presidential elections.

The essence of expected utility theory is a set of related assumptions about rational human behavior. Specifically, it is assumed that people:

- Are aware of the alternatives available to them for achieving a goal
- Order their preferences for these alternatives according to the **benefit** ("utility") to be gained from each
- Determine the **likelihood** that each alternative will occur (the "expected" part of expected utility)
- Weigh the potential benefit from each alternative according to its likely occurrence to determine the "expected utility" of each alternative
- Choose the alternative that has the highest expected utility.

In a simplified illustration of this more complex approach, to forecast the vote for president, the analyst first divides the electorate into major groupings, each of which is assumed to be mutually exclusive and to behave as a single entity. Groups thus are the "actors," or participants, in the electoral process. Next, an assessment is made of the *benefits* to each group of voting for each candidate. This entails identifying key interests important to the group, and then estimating the candidate's support for those interests. That is, to what extent does the candidate favor policies that are important to the group and would benefit it? As we see, making this determination is essentially a two-step process: identifying **salient issues** and their **relative importance** to the group, and determining the extent that the **candidate's stance** on those issues benefits the group.

For example, suppose that we identify older voters as a group—say, those 65 years of age and older. Let us assume that there are two issues important to people in this group. Of paramount importance is their economic well-being in this period of life when their earning power is low. They, therefore, favor government policies that maintain or improve the quality of their retired life, such as assured funding for the Social Security system, expanded health care benefits under Medicare, and the like. Also assume that these older voters, whose ethical beliefs were formed when traditional family-oriented values were more pervasive, continue to stress the importance of those values in dealing with social issues. The analyst must make a determination of the relative importance of these two areas of concern to older voters. Suppose it is determined that economic well-being is much more important to these voters than promoting traditional values. On a scale of 0 to 1, economic well-being rates .75, whereas traditional values rate .25.

Next, assume that two candidates are running for president, the Democrat and the Republican. The analyst determines that the position of the Democrat is more closely associated with older voters' economic interests, whereas the views of the Republican are more in accord with their ethical stance. On economic issues, the analyst believes that older voters would have much greater confidence in the Democrat's policies, rating the Democrat .7 and the Republican .3. On promoting traditional values older voters might favor the Republican somewhat more, rating that candidate .6 and the Democrat .4.

To determine the potential benefit of voting for the Democrat versus the Republican, the ratings of the issues' relative importance are merged with the issue positions of the candidates by multiplying them together, and then adding those results. These calculations are made in Table 5.6. The benefit of voting for the Democrat is determined to be .625, and .375 for the Republican. That is, on balance it is potentially more beneficial to older voters to vote for the Democrat. But that determination alone does not mean that they will vote in that way.

According to the theory, voters also take into account the *likelihood* of each candidate providing these benefits to them. This is primarily an assessment by the group of the strength of the candidacy of the Republican and the Democrat, as assessed by the analyst. What are their respective chances of being elected? A candidate's policies may be ideal for the group, but if there is no possibility of

Table 5.6 BENEFITS (UTILITIES) FOR OLDER VOTERS

	Importance of Issue to Group		Group's Agreement with Candidate's Position on Issue		Benefit of Voting for Candidate
Benefits from voting for **Democrat**					
Economic benefits	.75	×	.70	=	.525
Traditional values	.25	×	.40	=	.10
				Total benefits	.625
Benefits from voting for **Republican**					
Economic benefits	.75	×	.30	=	.225
Traditional values	.25	×	.60	=	.15
				Total benefits	.375

the candidate winning, the group will not benefit. Thus, an expectation of winning is factored into the calculations for the group. Trial heat polls are a readily available source for this estimate. Suppose that polls show that the Republican is leading the Democrat by 52 percent to 48 percent, and that this is the expected election result. What would older voters do? The Democrat would provide more benefits, but the Democrat may lose. To make this determination, the benefits to older voters accruing from the respective candidates would be adjusted by taking into account their expected election fortunes. This is done by multiplying potential benefits times the likelihood of winning for each candidate:

	Potential Benefits to Group	×	Likelihood of Candidate Winning	=	Expected Benefits to Group
The Democrat	.625	×	.48	=	**.30**
The Republican	.375	×	.52	=	**.195**

We see that the expected benefit (utility) of voting for the Democrat (.30) is somewhat greater than that of voting for the Republican (.195). Older voters thus would be assumed to vote for the Democrat.

To complete the expected utility analysis for older voters, we need to estimate the percentage of voters in the upcoming election that is likely to be from this group. This estimate could come from contemporaneous surveys of the electorate or from surveys made near the time of the previous mid-term election, such as the American National Election Studies. Suppose we find that this group comprises 15 percent of the electorate. If so, then 15 percent of the vote would be recorded as favoring the given candidate expected to produce the greatest benefits for this group.

In similar fashion, the expected benefits for other key groups in the electorate would be determined along with each group's share of the anticipated voters. The candidate then favored by groups representing a majority of the anticipated electorate would be forecast to win.

Conclusion

In this chapter, I have explored several techniques in which forecasts are derived from the informed judgment of experts. Some have been explicitly applied to forecasting past presidential elections; others have not. Those in the latter group, however, appear to be potentially useful in election forecasting.

The common criticism of judgment-based forecasts is that they introduce more bias into the analysis than do quantitative techniques. For example, prior to the 1992 election, political psychologist Philip Tetlock of Ohio State University and collaborator Aaron Belkin collected 34 expert predictions of the election outcome. They discovered that the experts were "no more accurate than one would expect from chance, evenly dividing . . . between Bush and Clinton. . . ." When the experts were contacted after the election, those who were correct, and even those who were not, continued to believe in the soundness of their judgments. Experts who wrongly predicted a Bush victory "were much more likely than those who foresaw a Clinton win to attribute the outcome to easily avoidable—and, by implication, utterly unforeseeable—tactical errors by the Bush campaign" (Tetlock and Belkin 1996b, 17–18). The experts' problem is with the crystal ball, not in their reading of it—according to the experts!

Budge and Farlie combined both approaches, judgment and quantitative analysis. Their use of regression for only nine cases (elections), however, likely did not reduce bias, and in fact led to wide confidence intervals for the two equations, which they report. Bias is probably best controlled by decomposing the forecast into smaller categories, analyzing and making predictions for each, as in the expected utility approach.

Expected utility theory is not without its critics, who in this context might ask: Are voters always rational, never being swayed by such irrational influences as the images and personalities of the candidates? Is it reasonable to assume that voters in groups defined by the analyst all vote for the same candidate? In response, expected utility theorists likely would admit to exceptions on both counts, but would contend that their assumptions apply to the great majority of voters in the respective groups. Moreover, any model of voting is only a partial description of the electoral process, and not every case can be expected to follow the pattern.

On balance, the forecasting record of judgment-based approaches is mixed, although the more successful techniques could be usefully applied to election forecasting more frequently than at present. Their greatest advantage lies in the possibility of explicitly incorporating into the analysis the expertise of knowledgeable experts whose depth of understanding of the electoral process can translate perceptive insights into effective forecasts.

Cycles in Presidential Elections

The two parties which divide the state,
the party of Conservatism and that of
Innovation, are very old, and have disputed
the possession of the world ever since it was
made . . . now one, now the other gets the
day, and still the fight renews itself as if
for the first time, under new names and
hot personalities.

Ralph Waldo Emerson
"The Conservative" (1841)

Some political observers have long suggested the existence of alternating patterns in politics that recur with some regularity. Do the outcomes of presidential elections follow any sort of cyclical pattern? Are Democratic administrations elected for X terms, followed by Republican administrations elected for Y (or X) terms, followed by Democratic administrations for X terms again? If such regularities exist, it would be possible to forecast presidential election outcomes according to where a particular election is in the cycle.

In pure cycle-based forecasting, no effort is made to take external causes into account. As historian Arthur Schlesinger, Jr., a proponent of this approach, states with reference to cycles in American politics:

> If it is a genuine cycle, the explanation must be primarily internal. Each new phase must flow out of the conditions—and contradictions—of the phase before and then itself prepare the way for the next recurrence. A true cycle, in other words, is self-generating. It cannot be determined, short of a catastrophe, by external events (Schlesinger, Jr. 1986, 27).

Schlesinger traces American observers of political cycles back to the last century, quoting Ralph Waldo Emerson (the epigram at the beginning of the chapter) and Henry Adams. Adams observed:

Experience seemed to show that a period of about twelve years measured the beat of the pendulum. After the Declaration of Independence, twelve years had been needed to create an efficient Constitution; another twelve years of energy brought a reaction against the government then created; a third period of twelve years was ending in a sweep toward still greater energy; and already a child could calculate the result of a few more such returns (Adams 1890, 123).

In this chapter, it will be apparent that cycles can be linked to presidential elections and can be useful in forecasting their outcomes. I begin by considering the relevance of alternating patterns of liberalism and conservatism, and of public purpose and private interest, identified by Schlesinger and his father. Then I note the tendency since World War II of parties to alternate in the White House every eight years, as well as long-term cyclical patterns in presidential elections existing since 1860. Finally, I consider the relevance of cyclical patterns in mid-term elections for forecasting presidential elections.

Cycles of Liberalism and Conservatism: Arthur M. Schlesinger, Sr.

In a 1924 lecture, Harvard historian Arthur M. Schlesinger, Sr., first articulated his conception that American history has been characterized by a systematic alternation between periods of liberalism and periods of conservatism (Schlesinger, Sr. 1949, 77–92). Writing in 1949, he observed the historical pattern reproduced in Table 6.1.

Table 6.1 ARTHUR SCHLESINGER, SR.'S POLITICAL CYCLES

Historical patterns observed by Schlesinger, Sr.:

1765–1787	liberal
1787–1801	conservative
1801–1816	liberal
1816–1829	conservative
1829–1841	liberal
1841–1861	conservative
1861–1869	liberal
1869–1901	conservative
1901–1919	liberal
1919–1931	conservative
1931–1947	liberal

Forecasts made by Schlesinger, Sr.:

1947–1962	conservative ("recession from liberalism")
1962–1978	liberal

Author's forecasts using median length of Schlesinger's historical periods:

1978–1992	conservative
1992–2008	liberal

Source for Schlesinger data: Schlesinger, Sr. (1949, 81, 85).

The average length of Schlesinger's five conservative periods, listed in the table, is 18.2 years. This average is boosted by the lengthy conservative periods in the last half of the nineteenth century. The conservative periods' median, a measure that minimizes the effect of extreme scores, is lower, 14 years. The average length of the six liberal periods is 15.1 years, with a median of 15.5 years.

In his 1949 predictions of future liberal and conservative periods, Schlesinger chooses period lengths that are close to the medians: " . . . we may expect the recession from liberalism, which began in 1947, to last till 1962 [15 years], with a possible margin of a year or two in one direction or the other. The next conservative epoch will then be due around 1978 [16 years]" (Schlesinger, Sr. 1949, 85).

If I use the 14-year median of the conservative time spans, the conservative period that Schlesinger forecast to begin in 1978 should have ended around 1992. The liberal period, which then would have begun at that point, should last until about 2008, given the 15.5 year median for liberal periods historically.

Although Schlesinger does not explicitly attempt to predict presidential elections, he does link periods of liberalism and conservatism to specific presidents and to the parties controlling Congress. In this century, liberal periods tend to have more Democratic presidents, whereas conservative periods bring more Republican presidents to power. If one can forecast the occurrence of a liberal or conservative period, then one also may be able to forecast the probable election of a Democratic or Republican president, respectively.

In fact, however, presidential administrations do not precisely coincide with the ideological periods. The 1947–1962 conservative period predicted by Schlesinger did include the status quo Eisenhower Administration—but it also included Truman and Kennedy. The 1962–1978 liberal period included the presidencies of Democrats Kennedy, Johnson, and Carter. Moreover, it included the civil rights revolution and major programs to alleviate poverty. But this liberal period also included Nixon and Ford, both Republicans.

On balance, Schlesinger's cyclical periods probably are more useful in identifying and predicting the political *mood* of the country than in forecasting which party will occupy the White House. It is, however, instructive that a 14-year conservative period beginning in 1978 was a period of Republican presidents (except for Carter's last two years). It also is noteworthy that a Democrat—Clinton—was elected in 1992, in what would be the beginning of a new liberal period. If Democrats are liberal and Republicans are conservative, we could infer from this pattern the implicit prediction of another Democratic president after Clinton, since the liberal period should last until 2008. Gore's close victory in the popular vote in 2000 provides support for this interpretation, although, of course, this outcome is counterbalanced by the Republican victory in the Electoral College.

Cycles of Public Purpose and Private Interest: Arthur M. Schlesinger, Jr.

Schlesinger's son, Arthur M. Schlesinger, Jr., later also identified political cycles alternating between what he calls periods of "public purpose and private interest," each lasting about 15 years (Schlesinger, Jr. 1986, Ch. 2).

Schlesinger explicitly builds on his father's work and echoes economist Albert O. Hirschman's view of the public-private dichotomy (Hirschman 1982). Schlesinger observes:

> As the private interest of the 1920s had led to the public action of the 1930s, the 1950s now led into the 1960s and a new rush of commitment . . . . By the later 1970s Americans were once more, as they had been in the 1950s and 1920s, fed up with public action and disenchanted by its consequences. The compass needle now swung toward private interest and the fulfillment of self. The time received its appropriate names—the "me" decade; the "culture of narcissism." The reaction reached its culmination in the age of Reagan in the 1980s (Schlesinger, Jr. 1986, 32).

Schlesinger, Jr., links cycles directly to presidential elections: "Each swing of the cycle produced Presidents responsive to the national mood. . . ." (1986, 32). Given a 15-year pattern, a period of public purpose would have been expected to arise in the mid-90s. Since he seems to link periods of "private interest" with Republican administrations and periods of "public purpose" with Democratic administrations, the Democratic administration of Bill Clinton in the 90s would fit the pattern. With Clinton's two terms accounting for only about half of the 15-year public-purpose period, the implicit prediction, seemingly, was for another Democrat to follow Clinton.

Two-Term Penalty

In 1988, political scientist Alan Abramowitz observed a tendency by the electorate to penalize a party that has occupied the White House for two consecutive terms, the "time for a change" phenomenon, as he dubbed it (Abramowitz 1988; 1996). Thus, the candidate of the incumbent president's party is likely to lose when a victory would result in a third consecutive term for that party.

Abramowitz did not consider this two-election indicator alone, but analyzed it jointly with others, which he also found to be significant in a multivariable regression. Statistically, the two-election indicator is a column of zeros and ones—ones for elections in which the president's party was finishing two terms; zeros for elections in which the president's party had not been in the White House that long. Thus, even though this phenomenon is a "two-term penalty," it is also a "one-term reward." That is, the candidate of the incumbent president's party—presumably the incumbent himself—running for a second consecutive term is likely to win. In this sense the phenomenon is **cyclical,** resulting in a tendency of the party in the White House to alternate every eight years. As seen in Table 6.2, the two-term penalty/one-term reward pattern correctly predicted the winner in 10 of the 13 elections from 1952 to 2000. The exceptions were 1980, when Carter would have been expected to win after serving only one term; and 1988 when Bush's election resulted in three consecutive terms for the Republicans. In terms of the popular vote, the 2000 election also is an exception to the two-term pattern, since Gore's close win was the third consecutive victory for the Democrats. Republican Bush's victory in the Electoral College, however, was consistent with the tendency toward party change.

Table 6.2 TWO-TERM PENALTY/ONE-TERM REWARD PHENOMENON

Election Year	Incumbent Party Candidate	Incumbent Party Ending Two or More Terms?	Outcome for Incumbent Party
1952	Stevenson	Yes	Lost
1956	Eisenhower	No	Won
1960	Nixon	Yes	Lost
1964	Johnson	No	Won
1968	Humphrey	Yes	Lost
1972	Nixon	No	Won
1976	Ford	Yes	Lost
1980	Carter	No	**LOST***
1984	Reagan	No	Won
1988	Bush	Yes	**WON***
1992	Bush	Yes	Lost
1996	Clinton	No	Won
2000	Gore	Yes	**WON***

*The 1980, 1988, and 2000 elections do not follow the pattern. On the basis of the popular vote the 2000 election is considered to be a "win" for Gore, although, of course, he lost in the Electoral College.

Brad Lockerbie (2000) varies this indicator somewhat by counting the number of consecutive *years* that the incumbent party has occupied the presidency—not merely whether that party is completing two or more *terms*. He then converts the number of years into logarithms. This results in the incumbent party suffering the greatest penalty when it has been in office two terms, with (only) a somewhat larger penalty for three terms. (The common log of 4 [years] = .6; log of 8 = .9; log of 12 = 1.08.) Lockerbie argues that this approach "take[s] into account the rapid drop in support early in an administration that is followed by a slow decline in support" (2000, 126). Like Abramowitz, Lockerbie does not use this indicator alone. But if we do so, we find that the Lockerbie data correctly classify the same elections as the Abramowitz approach depicted in Table 6.2.

My regression linking Lockerbie's indicator to the incumbent party's share of the two-party vote accounts for 39 percent of the variation in election results from 1956–1996. (Lockerbie's data set begins with 1956, one or two elections later than most other models.) Inserting data for 2000 into the equation, for the Democrats' eight years in office, a Gore victory is predicted with 50.5 percent of the two-party vote. Since Gore in fact received 50.3 percent, this forecast is a mere 0.2 percent in error and correctly identifies the winner of the popular vote—though it has a huge +/− 12.0 percent margin of error.

A Long-Term Approach to Two-Term Cycles

Cycles in presidential election outcomes also have been identified by political scientist Helmut Norpoth, using the statistical technique of autoregression. (See Glossary for a description.) In 1995, Norpoth observed that from 1860 through 1992 the Republican share of the two-party vote was autocorrelated, meaning that the vote in a given election was statistically related to the vote in previous elections. This phenomenon led to the cyclical characteristics that are obvious in Figure 6.1, especially during the twentieth century (Norpoth 1995).

Norpoth sought to account for the Republican vote in a given election on the basis of the Republican vote in the previous two elections. A somewhat altered version of the equation that he produced follows, with "RepVote" being the Republican share of the combined Republican and Democratic vote for president. "T" is the current election; "T-1" is the immediate prior election (four years previous); "T-2" is the second election prior (eight years previous); "53.5" is the equation's constant.

$$\text{RepVote}_T = .52\,\text{RepVote}_{T\text{-}1} - .55\,\text{RepVote}_{T\text{-}2} + 53.5$$

EQUATION 6.1

(In this equation, as published, Norpoth did not include a constant because he had adjusted the election results in his historical data set by subtracting the average of these election scores from each election result [Norpoth 1995, 206, Note 3]. I recomputed the equation without this adjustment, so that actual values for the Republican share of the two-party vote can be entered into the equation. Thus, a constant is included in this version of the model.)

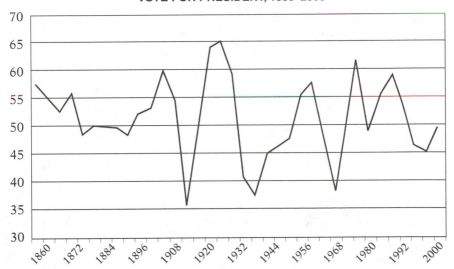

**REPUBLICAN PERCENTAGE OF MAJOR-PARTY
VOTE FOR PRESIDENT, 1860–2000**

Figure 6.1

SOURCE: Helmut Norpoth, "Is Clinton Doomed? An Early Forecast for 1996," *PS: Political Science & Politics* 28 (June 1995): 202. Copyright 1995 by the American Political Science Association. Reprinted by permission. [Data for 1996 and 2000 added by author.]

As evident in the equation, the election immediately prior is positively associated with the current election. That is, some factors that influenced the vote in the previous election continued to have similar influences in the current election.

Of particular interest to cycle theorists is Norpoth's second finding: The relationship between the current election and the election eight years ago— the second election prior—is *negative*. Recall that Norpoth is dealing with the percent of the vote received by the Republican candidate, not merely whether the candidate won or lost. Thus, we can say only that if the Republican candidate did well eight years ago, the Republican candidate in the current election likely would do less well. In Norpoth's scheme, this does not mean that the Republican necessarily would lose the current election, because the relationship to the prior election (T-1) is positive, which might counterbalance the negative effect of the election eight years ago (T-2).

Using his model, Norpoth forecast the 1996 election outcome. If the Republican percentages of the two-party vote in 1988 and 1992 (53.90 and 46.54, respectively) are substituted into the equation, the Republican—Dole— would garner 47.7 percent of the two-party vote in 1996. (The 47.7% result is correct, although rounding errors throw off calculations made from the data presented by 0.3%.) That, of course, means that the Democrat—Clinton— would win, with 52.3 percent of the two-party vote (Norpoth 1995; 1996). In fact, Clinton received 54.7 percent of the two-party vote, resulting in a forecast error of 2.4 percent. As Norpoth notes, he could have made that forecast immediately after the 1992 election, since the only data required were available then: election results from 1992 (T-1) and 1988 (T-2).

Updating the data set to include the 1996 election, I proceeded in like manner to forecast the election in 2000 (which Norpoth also did with a similar result [2000a, 77, 81]). To do this, I recomputed the data, and then inserted into the new equation 1996 and 1992 Republican shares of the two-party vote (45.26% and 46.54%, respectively):

$$
\begin{aligned}
\textbf{Rep. Vote} \\
\text{in } \textbf{2000} \quad &= (.5322 \times 1996 \text{ Rep. Vote}) - (.5669 \times 1992 \text{ Rep. Vote}) + 53.1936 \\
&= (.5322 \times 45.26) - (.5669 \times 46.54) + 53.1936 \\
&= \textbf{50.9\%}
\end{aligned}
$$

EQUATION 6.2

The resulting forecasts predicted a very close election: a Republican win with 50.9 percent of the two-party vote. Given that Republican Bush received 49.7 percent of the vote, this prediction was only **1.2 percent in error**—remarkably close for a prediction *four years* prior to the election. However, the 95 percent confidence interval for the prediction is +/− 10.7 percent, which is not surprising, since the equation accounts for only 39 percent of the variation in the vote among the historical elections. In the data set, the average difference between the actual election results and estimates from the model is 9.3 percent.

In a variation of this approach, Norpoth (2000b) extended the data set back to the 1828 election. The resulting equation explained only 29 percent of the variation in the vote, on an adjusted basis. However, in a prediction of the 2000 election, Gore was forecast to receive 49.8 percent of the two-party vote, a difference of only 0.5 percent from his actual share, 50.3 percent. Norpoth's more elaborate forecasting models are described in Chapter 9.

Mid-Term Elections

Another cyclical pattern that has affected presidential elections is mid-term elections in the House of Representatives. These elections are "mid-term" in the sense that they fall in the middle of a president's four-year term, and they involve all members of the House, who all serve two-year terms.

Mid-term elections in the House are cyclical in two ways: First, the incumbent president's party nearly always fares worse in a mid-term election than in the previous presidential election, which thereby creates a two-year pattern of alternation. Second, the extent of mid-term decline that the president's party faces tends to alternate among successive mid-term elections—thus a four-year pattern of alternation.

The latter pattern, of greater interest for our purposes, is evident in observing the number of **seats lost** by the president's party in mid-term elections (Lewis-Beck and Rice 1992). As apparent in Figure 6.2, during much of the period of this study, 1952–2000, an alternation has occurred in which a

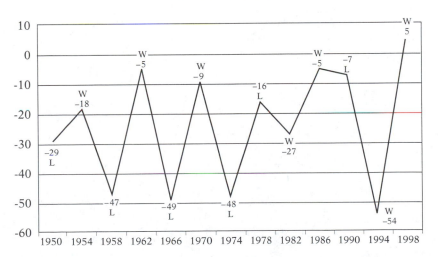

**SEATS LOST BY PRESIDENT'S PARTY
IN MID-TERM ELECTIONS**

W = Win for candidate of incumbent president's party two years later

L = Loss for candidate of incumbent president's party two years later

2000 is popular vote "win"

Figure 6.2

DATA SOURCES: U.S. Bureau of the Census (1975; 1996; 2000)

mid-term election having a large seat loss is followed four years later by a mid-term election with a smaller seat loss, in turn followed by a relatively larger seat loss at the next mid-term election. In Figure 6.3, we see that this pattern of alternation also is evident in changes in the share of total **votes** that House candidates of the president's party receive in mid-term elections. (Rosenstone [1983] uses this indicator at the state level.) For both indicators, seat loss and House votes, exceptions to the pattern occur at the end of the series, notably the 1990 and 1994 mid-term elections. The five-seat *gain* by the president's party in 1998 was unprecedented in recent mid-term election history. Perhaps in part it was a natural rebound from the party's exceptionally large loss of seats four years earlier.

Given the cyclical nature of the fortunes of the president's party in the House, is this phenomenon useful in forecasting presidential elections? As seen in Figures 6.2 and 6.3, prior to 1978, the four-year pattern of alternation among mid-term elections was consistent, as was its relationship to presidential elections. A large seat loss or a large percentage drop in House votes by the president's party at mid-term predicted a loss by the candidate of the president's party two years later. Conversely, a small seat loss or a small percentage drop in House votes by the president's party at the mid-term election predicted a victory for the presidential candidate of the incumbent party.

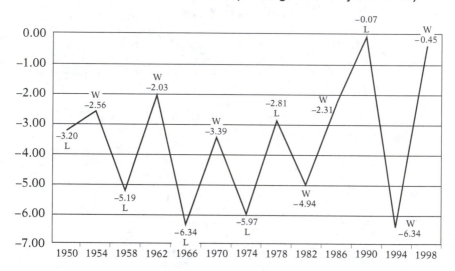

**NATIONAL VOTE FOR INCUMBENT PRESIDENT'S PARTY
IN MID-TERM HOUSE ELECTIONS (% change from two years earlier)**

W = Win for candidate of incumbent
president's party two years later

L = Loss for candidate of incumbent
president's party two years later

2000 is popular vote "win"

Figure 6.3

DATA SOURCES: U.S. Bureau of the Census (1975; 1996; 2000)

Beginning in 1978, however, the link to presidential elections appeared to reverse, which is most evident in the data on House votes—Figure 6.3. When the president's party performed better in mid-term elections, it tended to *lose* the presidential election two years later; and when it did worse at mid-term it tended to *win* the White House in two years. (Exceptions to this reverse pattern occurred in 1986 and 1998.)

Reasonable explanations can be offered to account for the differing win-loss relationships between mid-term elections and presidential elections. As to the pre-1978 pattern, when the president's party does well at mid-term, that may be evidence of growing support for that party, which carries over two years later in the presidential election, resulting in a victory. On the other hand, the post-1978 pattern leads us to the argument of Alesina, Londregan, and Rosenthal (1996), who contend that voters consciously vote to increase or decrease the strength of the president's opposition party in Congress as needed to counterbalance the power of the president. As they argue,

> middle-of-the-road voters take advantage of this form of "checks and balances" to achieve moderation and, for this reason, some of them favor the party not holding the Presidency in congressional elections. Conversely, if incumbency advantage in the House and Senate gives one party a grip on these institutions, the voters may favor the other party in presidential elections (1996, 116–117).

Alesina and his collaborators found evidence of this phenomenon during 1918–1994 in regression equations using as an indicator the incumbent president's share of seats in the House. In the 1952–2000 period under study here, the pre- and post–1978 patterns appear in the figures visually, to the extent noted previously. The results of my regressions testing the relationships statistically, however, were not significant. (In one regression, the vote share of the incumbent party's presidential candidate was regressed on that party's share of the total vote for House candidates in mid-term elections, controlling for pre- and post-1978 mid-term elections with a dummy variable. In another regression, seat loss in the House by the incumbent president's party was substituted for that party's House votes.)

Conclusion

The cyclical approaches described in this chapter are a diverse group. Some are highly impressionistic; others are mathematical. All of them, however, reflect this common theme: Identifiable patterns of alternation—cycles—exist in American politics which are relevant to predicting presidential elections.

The Schlesingers, Jr. and Sr., observed periodic changes in the mood of the country, generally lasting about 15 years, which can be loosely linked to the alternation of parties winning the presidency. Abramowitz found that, since World War II, parties occupying the White House for two terms tend to be turned out by voters, rather than returned for a third term. Lockerbie's results were compatible with these findings. Norpoth's work, covering 140 years, similarly captured the cyclical tendency of voters to change presidential parties after eight years and the companion tendency not to do so after four years.

The final cyclical patterns appearing in the chapter link mid-term elections in the House to the results of presidential elections. As we observed, the president's party tends to perform better in mid-term elections every eight years than it does in the intervening mid-term elections. Between 1952 and 1978 when the president's party did well at mid-term that party won the presidency two years later, and it lost the White House when it did poorly. Since 1978 the reverse pattern has occurred, although less consistently.

On balance, each of these approaches has been useful in forecasting presidential elections. But none is accurate all of the time, which suggests that elections do not invariably follow predetermined cyclical patterns.

7
★ ★ ★

The Nomination Process and Campaigns

The journey is the reward.

Zen slogan

Do the presidential nominating process and campaign activities provide clues as to the likely winner in an upcoming election for president? In particular, can an election outcome be predicted from the extent of the party nominees' success in primary elections, from activities surrounding nominating conventions, or from the post-convention campaign? In this short chapter, I address these three issues.

Primary Elections

Some researchers have suggested that the success of a party's nominee for president in primary elections has a bearing on that candidate's later success in the general election and can aid in forecasting the outcome. Helmut Norpoth (1996) has observed a link between victory in the first presidential primary and winning the presidency. Michael Lewis-Beck and Tom Rice, on the other hand, have proposed that the share of the vote received by the incumbent party candidate in all primary elections is positively related to that candidate's share of the electoral vote in the general election (1992, 52).

The latter indicator, incumbent vote share in all primaries (converted to a dummy variable), was included in a multi-variable model that proved unsuccessful in forecasting the 1992 election. In a later collaboration, Lewis-Beck, working with Charles Tien (1996), dropped this variable from a revised, successful forecasting model for the 1996 election. The use of the vote in all primaries as an indicator seems inherently flawed because presidential primary elections have not been of uniform importance throughout the historical period included in post–World War II models. A much larger percentage of the electorate participates in primaries today than in 1948 or 1952. This is because the number of states in which delegates to the national conventions are chosen in primaries, rather than by state conventions, has increased significantly since then. For this reason, I do not pursue this indicator further.

Norpoth's emphasis on the first primary is based on the assumption that important clues of a candidate's future electoral performance are evident in that early election. Failure to win the first primary may be indicative of the candidate's weak voter appeal, of division within the party, or perhaps of weak campaign organization. On the other hand, if the party nominee wins the first presidential primary, these problems likely do not exist, and that candidate will be more likely to win the general election, *if* the opposing party's candidate lost the first primary. If both parties' nominees won the first presidential primary, or if neither did, there is no impact on the general election. In those circumstances, the indicator does not apply.

Although Norpoth reviews the first presidential primaries since 1912, only those from 1952 onward are reported in Table 7.1. I have made this choice because 1952 marks the beginning of the period in which the New Hampshire primary has consistently been the first such election of the campaign season. For these primaries in New Hampshire, the Norpoth hypothesis was confirmed in eight of the 13 elections from 1952 through 2000. Results in four of the 13 were inconclusive because both parties' candidates won their party's first presidential primary, so neither had an advantage. The hypothesis was not confirmed in 1992, when Bush incorrectly was predicted to win reelection. Bush won the first Republican primary, whereas Clinton, the Democratic nominee, failed to win his party's first primary. Thus, Bush should have won the general election, but, of course, did not. This scheme was correct in forecasting the 1996 election outcome, since Clinton won the New Hampshire primary, and Dole did not. In 2000, Gore, the Democratic nominee, won the New Hampshire primary, defeating Bradley. But George W. Bush, the Republican candidate, lost in New Hampshire to challenger John McCain. This indicator, therefore, predicted a Gore victory over Bush, which, in terms of the popular vote, occurred.

On balance, the first primary indicator is remarkably accurate, to be as simple as it is. The main drawback is that it is not applicable to a sizable proportion of presidential contests. In nearly one-third of the elections since 1952, nominees of both major parties won their first primaries, with neither having an advantage over the other.

Disorderly Conventions

Norman Ornstein, scholar at the American Enterprise Institute, boldly states: "The single most powerful predictor of presidential election outcomes is how smoothly the parties' conventions run" (1995, 51). Disruptive conventions, he argues, are evidence of intra-party divisions, which make it difficult for all elements within the party to unite behind the nominee. Disruptive conventions also reflect badly on the party in the eyes of the electorate, especially those watching on television. They project the image of a party that lacks sufficient unity to govern, and thus turn voters away. The party that has the least disruptive, least controversial, well-run nominating

Table 7.1 WINNERS OF FIRST PRIMARY (NEW HAMPSHIRE)

Year	Prediction Correct?	Incumbent Party	Challenger Party
1952	Correct	Kefauver (D) [Stevenson]	EISENHOWER (R)
1956	Correct	EISENHOWER (R)	Kefauver (D) [Stevenson]
1960	Inconclusive	NIXON (R)	KENNEDY (D)
1964	Correct	JOHNSON (D)	Lodge (R) [Goldwater]
1968	Correct	Johnson (D) [Humphrey]	NIXON (R)
1972	Correct	NIXON (R)	Muskie (D) [McGovern]
1976	Inconclusive	FORD (R)	CARTER (D)
1980	Inconclusive	CARTER (D)	REAGAN (R)
1984	Correct	REAGAN (R)	Hart (D) [Mondale]
1988	Inconclusive	BUSH (R)	DUKAKIS (D)
1992	Incorrect	BUSH (R)	Tsongas (D) [Clinton]
1996	Correct	CLINTON (D)	Buchanan (R) [Dole]
2000	Correct*	GORE (D)*	McCain (R) [Bush]

Name in CAPS: winner of first primary; and won party's nomination.
Name underlined: winner of election.
*Gore, winner of the popular vote in 2000, is for this purpose treated as the election "winner."
Name in lowercase, not brackets: winner of first primary; but did NOT win party nomination.
Name in brackets: NOT winner of first primary; but won party nomination.
(D) denotes Democrat; (R) denotes Republican.

Source: Adapted from Helmut Norpoth, "Of Time and Candidates: A Forecast for 1996," *American Politics Quarterly* vol. 24, no. 4, October 1996, p. 464. Copyright by Sage Publications, Inc. Reprinted by permission of Sage Publications, Inc. [1996 and 2000 data added by author]

convention does not suffer from these negative influences and thus is more likely to win the presidency.

For evidence of this proposition, Ornstein refers to national party conventions from 1964 through 1992. For example, in 1964, Democrats easily unified behind Johnson, while "Goldwater conservatives [were] booing Rockefeller moderates off the podium and near fistfights [occurred] on the floor" (1995, 51). Johnson, of course, won. In 1968, the Democratic convention was one of the most raucous in recent history, leaving Humphrey's party in disarray. The late James Reston, famed reporter and editor for the *New York Times*, recalled:

> There the demonstrators were not only numerous but frantic, and while the
> gentle mayor and his minions didn't shoot to kill, they gave the impression

Table 7.2 ORNSTEIN'S ANALYSIS OF DISORDERLY NATIONAL PARTY CONVENTIONS

	Party with Most Disorderly Convention (Candidate)	Source of Disorder	Party Winning Election (Winning Candidate)
1964	Republican (Goldwater)	Friction between Goldwater conservatives and Rockefeller moderates	Democrat (Johnson)
1968	Democrat (Humphrey)	Anti-Vietnam War sentiment	Republican (Nixon)
1972	Democrat (McGovern)	Antagonism between backers of McGovern and Humphrey	Republican (Nixon)
1976	Republican (Ford)	Close competition for nomination between Ford and Reagan	Democrat (Carter)
1980	Democrat (Carter)	Dominance of challenger Ted Kennedy at convention	Republican (Reagan)
1984	Democrat (Mondale)	Dominance of Mario Cuomo at convention	Republican (Reagan)
1988	Democrat (Dukakis)	Jesse Jackson platform floor fight	Republican (Bush)
1992	Republican (Bush)	High profile of right wing especially Pat Buchanan	Democrat (Clinton)

Data Source: Ornstein (1995).

outside the hall that they might, and the disorder inside the convention was almost as bad. In the end, the delegates nominated Hubert Humphrey, and later, in trying to analyze how on earth he ever lost to Nixon, I concluded that the voters watching this outrageous Democratic party performance on television had decided then and there that if the Democrats couldn't govern themselves, why take a chance on them governing the country (Reston 1992, 361)?

In contrast, "the Republican convention was a sterile but tranquil polar opposite" (Ornstein 1995, 51). The Republican, Nixon, won in a close race.

Ornstein provides similar analyses for other national conventions through 1992, as summarized in Table 7.2. He observes that in 1992 the Democratic convention "was as tightly orchestrated as any Democratic convention since LBJ's in [1964]." On the other hand, Bush's Republican convention was "rife with ideological tension, and the most riveting moment by far was the prime-time speech of Pat Buchanan—a right-wing, take-no-prisoners clarion call" (1995, 52).

The problem with this approach is that the reader is not given a good indicator of disruption or turmoil. How does one assess the extent of disorder at a convention? How much disarray will lead to an election loss? How much is too much? Where is the threshold? Ornstein does not say. Thus, the approach is impressionistic. In any case, this may all be beside the point because party nominations are now usually decided well ahead of the convention in the primary campaign. The convention then becomes a coronation of the preselected candidate, with little chance of a disorderly convention, as true in 1996 and 2000.

Post-Convention Campaigns

In 1996, Thomas Holbrook, referring to post-convention fall presidential campaigns, published a book with the intriguing title: *Do Campaigns Matter?* (1996a). Intuitively, one responds that of course campaigns matter (Campbell 2000a, 4, 186). Certainly most journalists believe that they matter, as they follow the fall campaign horse race in excruciating detail. The public seems to believe that they matter, as they—the attentive public, at least—follow the media coverage that journalists provide. Above all, the candidates believe that they matter, judging from the physical ordeal they are willing to endure and the millions of dollars they spend during a campaign.

However, Holbrook's question is a pertinent one because various indicators, the data for which are available in the pre-campaign summer or late spring, can often predict the November election outcome with considerable accuracy. Some of these variables have been discussed in previous chapters; others will be considered in chapters that follow. If indicators available prior to the fall campaign can predict the election result, then it would seem that the fall campaign must not be an important influence on voters. This is not a new idea. Pioneering research by Paul Lazarsfeld and colleagues in Erie County, Ohio, in 1940 showed that elections there were largely decided by Labor Day (Lazarsfeld, Berelson, and Gaudet 1944).

In thorough tests of this question, Holbrook demonstrates that factors other than the campaign ("national conditions") have much greater impact on elections than does the campaign (1996a, 146). His primary conclusion, however, is that campaigns do have some significant influences on election outcomes that can be documented, particularly among people who change their preferences for candidates. Moreover, it may be that the true impact of campaigns on elections is greater than the campaign influences that can be readily measured. Some evidence exists that campaigns provide essential information to voters, enabling them to assess the state of the economy and other pertinent conditions (Gelman and King 1993; Holbrook 1996a).

In a more recent comprehensive study of campaigns, James Campbell finds that since World War II "campaigns on average have made a difference of about **four percentage points** in the vote and have been decisive in perhaps one in every five or six elections. . . ." (2000a, 193 [emphasis added]). But Campbell, like Holbrook, believes that campaigns are more important than such figures suggest.

To a great extent, Campbell (2000a) contends, factors that influence elections do so because they influence campaigns, which in turn influence election results. In his view the course that a campaign takes is largely determined by circumstances that exist before the campaign begins: the tendency of people to vote for the candidate of their party, the health of the economy, whether the president is running for reelection. These factors shape the campaign, which in turn affects voters' choices and thus the election outcome. For example, the

health of the economy is routinely an important issue in presidential campaigns, which in turn triggers voter evaluations of the economy, thereby affect-
ing electoral support for the incumbent party candidate. In essence, the
campaign is the conduit through which these influences impact the election.

Analysts know from studying past campaigns the likely effect of pre-
campaign influences. Thus one should be able to predict how a given campaign will unfold by observing the state of the economy and other influences.
Furthermore, because the campaign in turn affects the election, one should
also be able to predict the election result from these same factors that impact
the campaign.

Some influences on the election originate within the campaign—and thus
are independent of pre-campaign influences. For example, campaigns produce intense competition between the major-party candidates, which focuses
voters' attention and progressively narrows the differences in support for the
candidates, producing a closer election than anticipated before the campaign.
These effects of competition tend to occur in all presidential campaigns, so
they, too, are predictable, like the pre-campaign influences. However, influences that originate within the campaign have much less impact on the election outcome than do pre-campaign factors.

What does Campbell's argument—as I have interpreted it—mean for the
election forecaster? Normally it is not necessary to take campaigns into
account to accurately predict presidential election outcomes. The forecaster
can concentrate on analyzing the pre-campaign influences, which can predict
both campaign effects and election results. The influences that originate
within campaigns, which have an average 4 percent effect on elections, can
usually be set aside.

However, campaigns can make a significant difference in close elections,
as in 1948, 1960, and 2000. This possibility suggests that the forecaster might
be well advised to include a campaign indicator in his or her work, even if only
as a check on models using pre-campaign variables. Trial heat polls are an
obvious choice. Chapter 1 demonstrates the relationship between election
results and trial heats made at several points during the campaign. Campbell
(1996) has used this approach in multi-variable models. (An assessment of the
2000 campaign and election appears in the Conclusion to the book.)

Conclusion

We see that the contribution of the nomination process and of campaigns to
forecasting presidential elections is mixed. A party nominee who has won the
New Hampshire primary when his opponent has not is much more likely to
win the presidency. The absence of a disruptive nominating convention may
foretell victory for a party's nominee, especially if the opposing party has experienced a disruptive convention. Increasingly, however, this indicator may be
of only historic interest, since nomination contests are now over by convention time. Finally, fall presidential campaigns typically have only a limited
independent effect on election results. Thus it is usually not necessary to
account for campaign factors in predicting the outcome of an election.

Performance
of the Economy

It's the Economy, Stupid!

—James Carville (1992)

It's Still *the Economy, Stupid!*

—James Carville (1996)

We know from existing research—and political consultant James Carville's pithy aphorisms—that the state of the national economy has an important influence on presidential election outcomes. In particular, voters tend to hold the incumbent president responsible for economic conditions, whether in the past or expected in the future, and with their votes reward or punish the president and his party accordingly (Fiorina 1981; Kinder and Kiewiet 1981, Markus 1988, Holbrook 1991).

If economic conditions prior to the election are good or if the economy is expected to be robust in the future, voters will likely retain the incumbent president's party in the White House. This seems to be true whether the president himself is running for reelection or someone else is the candidate of his party. Conversely, if economic conditions prior to the election are poor or if economic prospects for the future are bleak, voters will turn the president's party out of the White House. If these assumptions have a familiar ring, they are similar to those underlying the use of presidential approval ratings in forecasting presidential elections, discussed in Chapter 3, in which voters reward or punish the candidate of the president's party on the basis of overall presidential performance, not merely the economy.

Various indicators of economic conditions have been used by analysts in efforts to forecast presidential elections. Most reflect *past* economic conditions and assume that voters take a retrospective view of the economy, judging the incumbent administration on the basis of past economic performance. Among such indicators are economic growth rates, interest rates, and surveys of current economic well-being compared with that in the past. By contrast, other studies assume that voters take a prospective view of the economy rather than looking to the past. These use measures of anticipated *future* economic conditions, gleaned from surveys of the public's expectations or from leading economic indicators.

In this chapter, I review economic indicators that have been important in the literature on presidential election forecasting and assess their impact on election outcomes. As originally presented, nearly all of these indicators were used in combination with other variables in multiple regressions, which will be described in the next chapter. In this analysis, however, they are considered individually.

As in previous chapters, I use two approaches to link economic indicators to election outcomes, which in turn can enable us to make election forecasts. First, line plots are presented, which graphically compare values of an indicator prior to an election with the election result. In each case, the goal is to identify a "win" threshold beyond which an indicator is associated with victory for the candidate of the president's party and a "loss" threshold defining the point at which the candidate tends to lose. The five line plots reported are for indicators believed to best illustrate this approach. In four of them, only one election is misclassified by the win-loss cutpoints.

I again turn to regression equations for the second forecasting approach. Equations have been computed for each economic indicator described in the chapter. However, I report only the stronger equations, those in which an indicator can account for about half, or more, of the variation in election results for the 1952–1996 period. Equations for five indicators meet this criterion, although two are omitted due to problems with autocorrelation, thus leaving the three that I use to generate predictions of the 2000 election.

Retrospective Indicators

Indicators of past economic conditions that are prominent in the literature on forecasting presidential elections include: GDP and GNP measures of overall growth in the economy, growth in income, interest rates, survey of current personal finances, and stock market performance.

Overall Economic Growth

Measures of growth of the economy commonly appear in statistical efforts to forecast presidential elections. These include percent change in gross domestic product (GDP) (Abramowitz 1996; Campbell 1996) and gross national product (GNP) (Lewis-Beck and Rice 1992; Lewis-Beck and Tien 1996; Norpoth 1996), as well as those two indicators adjusted on a per capita basis (Lewis-Beck 1985; Lewis-Beck and Rice 1984). The time intervals for these indicators have varied. Political scientists tend to use data available well before the November election: the second quarter of the election year (Campbell 1996; Lewis-Beck and Rice 1984) or the first half of that year (Abramowitz 1996; Lewis-Beck and Rice 1992; Lewis-Beck and Tien 1996). The most prominent election forecaster among economists, Ray Fair of Yale University, currently includes in his models economic growth for the first three quarters of the election year, after having used second and third quarter data in earlier studies. A few researchers have used economic growth for the entire election year (Alesina, Londregan, and Rosenthal 1996; Norpoth 1996).

The use of indicators that include data for the third and fourth quarters presents an obvious forecasting problem. Data for the third quarter normally are not available from the releasing agency, the Commerce Department's Bureau of Economic Analysis (BEA), until the end of October, a few days before the election. (Releases of new data are reported on the BEA Web site at **http://www.bea.doc.gov.**) An election prediction with more lead time necessitates using a forecast of third quarter economic growth, which adds increased error to the election forecast. Models relying on economic growth for the entire election year include not only data that must be forecast, but also data that occur during the two months following the election, and thus logically could not be a cause of its outcome. For these reasons, indicators of growth in the third and fourth quarters are not pursued further in this chapter.

Although GDP or GNP growth are among the strongest indicators in multivariable regressions of presidential elections for 1952–1992, alone their performance is less than impressive. As evident from its r^2 value, second quarter GDP growth accounts for 38 percent of the variation in the election results over this period. Similarly, growth in the first half explains 31 percent.

Figure 8.1 graphically demonstrates the linkage between election outcomes and economic growth, using second quarter GDP data. (Results for the first half are similar.) These data normally are available at the end of July, about three months before the election. With the exception of one year, 1968, GDP growth has correctly differentiated between elections won and lost by the candidate of the president's party. As Figure 8.1 reveals, if second quarter GDP grows at an annual rate of only 1.5 percent, or lower, the incumbent party historically has lost the White House. However, if second quarter GDP growth is at least 2.6 percent, annualized, the incumbent party has won. Thus, a **1.5 percent** growth rate appears to be the **loss threshold**, whereas **2.6 percent** is the **win threshold**. (Growth rates between the win-loss thresholds are inconclusive.) As evident in the figure, the victory for incumbent President Clinton in 1996 would have been correctly predicted on this basis, since the 4.6 percent annualized GDP growth rate in the second quarter of 1996 exceeded the win threshold of 2.6 percent. Likewise, in 2000, the 5.6 percent second quarter growth rate would have predicted Vice President Gore's victory in the popular vote.

Growth in Income

An early user of growth in personal income as an indicator for forecasting presidential elections was Douglas Hibbs (1982; 1987), then of Harvard University, now at Goteborg University in Sweden. Specifically, Hibbs calculated a weighted average version of change in real disposable personal income per capita, which was cumulated over the 15 quarters of the incumbent president's

GDP GROWTH 2ND QUARTER
Annualized Percentage Change

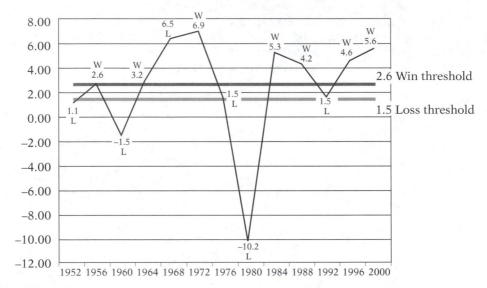

W = Win for candidate of incumbent   L = Loss for candidate of incumbent
      president's party   president's party

1968 is misclassified
2000 is popular vote "win"

Figure 8.1

DATA SOURCE: U.S. Bureau of Economic Analysis (2001)

term excluding the last quarter. In his scheme, each quarter counts 80 percent as much as the quarter that follows it. Since the inverse of .8 is 1.25, each successive quarter is given a weight 1.25 greater than the prior quarter. Data in recent quarters, therefore, have much greater impact on the indicator than data in early quarters. In fact, data for the quarter prior to an election are weighted 22.7 times more than data in the first quarter of the president's term, 15 quarters earlier.

Hibbs's election predictions have been generated by linking the vote to this income indicator alone. Recent forecasts from his model—and others— are reported on the Web site of John Irons (**http://economics.about.com/ money/economics/library/weekly/aa073100.htm**). According to Irons's original MIT Web site, Hibbs is reported to have correctly predicted the 1992 and 1996 election outcomes (although forecasts of third quarter income growth in the election years obviously were necessary). In 1996, in fact, he missed the mark by a slim 1.12 percent (**http://www.mit.edu/people/irons/myjava/ ecalc.html**). Hibbs's projections for the 2000 election—about 54 percent for Gore—and a detailed description of his method appear on his Web site (**http://cent.hgus.gu.se/~econdhib/election/index.php3**).

This approach for measuring income was adopted, with some changes, by Wlezien and Erikson. For one of their 1996 models, they chose income cumulated for the first 13 quarters of the incumbent president's term, ending March 31 of election years (Wlezien and Erikson 1996, 496). In this study I have found that, when used alone, the cumulative index of income growth for the first 14 quarters provides a better fit than that for 13 quarters. It accounts for nearly half of the variation in election outcomes (47%) from 1952 through 1996, compared to 29 percent for a 13-quarter equation. Line plots linking the 14-quarter cumulative income data with election results had two misclassified elections. The 13-quarter data plot had three elections wrongly classified.

Following is the regression equation linking 14-quarter cumulative income to election results for the 1952-1996 period. An after-the-fact forecast of the 2000 election is calculated by inserting the cumulative income value for that year into the equation.

incumbent (**Gore**)
share of two-party $= 45.266 + (1.088 \times \text{cumulative income growth}_{14\ \text{quarters}})$
vote in **2000**

$$= 45.266 + (1.088 \times 3.759)$$

$$= \mathbf{49.4\%}$$

EQUATION 8.1

r^2 .47 (.41 adjusted)   Durbin-Watson score 2.243
t-value 2.955   standard error of estimate 4.785
  (significance .01)   number of elections 12 (1952–1996)

This prediction of Gore garnering 49.4 percent of the two-party vote was only **0.9 percent in error**, given than Gore actually received 50.3 percent. The forecast margin of error, however, is very large, $+/-11.4$ percent.

Lockerbie (2000) used an income indicator presented in a form more similar to the gross product indicators described in the previous section than to the cumulative income variable shown in the preceding equation. Lockerbie simply calculated the percent change over a given period, specifically, change in real disposable personal income per capita from the second quarter of the year prior to the election to the second quarter of the election year (i.e., July through June).

Entering the data in a line plot shown in Figure 8.2, I discovered that when per capita personal income during this yearlong period rose 1.3 percent or more, the candidate of the incumbent president's party won in all but one election from 1952 through 2000. When income grew at a bit slower rate, 1.1 percent, the incumbent party candidate lost. (The election of 1968 was incorrectly classified as a win.) Thus, **1.3 percent** appears to be the **win threshold**, and **1.1 percent the loss threshold**. The elections of 1996 and 2000 would have been correctly predicted as popular vote victories for the incumbent Democratic party, given that income in those years rose 2.0 percent and 2.2 percent, respectively, which is above the win threshold.

A regression of income growth from mid-year to mid-year accounts for 51 percent of the variation in election outcomes from 1952 through 1996. The

REAL DISPOSABLE PERSONAL INCOME PER CAPITA
Percent Change, 2nd Quarter Prior Year to 2nd Quarter Election Year

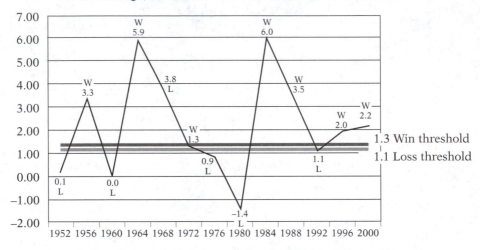

W = Win for candidate of incumbent   L = Loss for candidate of incumbent
        president's party   president's party

1968 is misclassified
2000 is popular vote "win"

Figure 8.2

DATA SOURCE: U.S. Bureau of Economic Analysis (2001)

income growth rate for this period in 2000, 2.2 percent, is entered into the equation to generate an *ex post* forecast for the 2000 election.

incumbent **(Gore)**
share of two-party = $48.502 + (1.916 \times \text{income growth}_{\text{mid-year to mid-year}})$
vote in 2000

$$= 48.502 + (1.916 \times 2.187)$$

$$= \textbf{52.7\%}$$

EQUATION 8.2

r^2 .51 (.46 adjusted)   Durbin-Watson score 2.789 (inconclusive)
t-value 3.197   standard error of estimate 4.605
   (significance .01)   number of elections 12 (1952–1996)

The prediction for Gore, 52.7 percent, was **2.4 percent off** from Gore's actual 50.3 percent share of the two-party vote in 2000. Again, the margin of error for the forecast is large, +/−10.7 percent.

Interest Rates

Interest rates are used to predict presidential election results in these published works: a book by stock market analyst Dick Stoken (1990) and an article by political economists Brian Berry, Euel Elliott, and Edward Harpham (1996).

Long-Term Corporate Rates

Stoken reports a link between interest rates, measured by rates for AAA corporate bonds, and presidential election outcomes:

> When long-term rates are low on November 15 twelve months before a presidential election, . . . it's a pretty safe bet that on election day the economy will be pulsating with energy. . . . People will be content with their lot, and the president—and his party—will be popular. . . .
>
> On the other hand, when long-term rates are high on that crucial day a year before the election, . . . the economy will lose its zip, and a wave of discontent is likely to sweep across the land—the mood of the country will be bitter on election day. This, of course, usually spells trouble for the party controlling the White House (Stoken 1990, 159–160).

Stoken then explains his means of determining when rates are high and low:

> Long-term rates will be considered high from the time they make a seven-year high until they fall back into another fifteen month low. . . . Long-term rates will be considered low from the time they make a fifteen-month low until a subsequent seven-year high is made (Stoken 1990, 160).

An update of Stoken's data for this study reveals that his scheme correctly identified the winning party in 11 of the 12 elections from 1952 through 1996; the 1992 election result was misclassified. However, given that the Stoken technique is not easily amenable to statistical analysis, I have sought to simplify his interest rate indicator, while preserving the essence of the concept. The indicator that I use is "yield on new high-grade corporate bonds" from November three years prior to the election (T-3) through November of the year before the election (T-1). The change in these interest rates over that period is calculated. Data closer to the election than one year prior are not used because of the delayed impact of rates on economic activity and thus presumably on voter opinion.

The link between bond rates and election results is negative because high interest rates lead to unemployment and other economic problems, which voters tend to lay at the feet of the incumbent president. This inverse relationship is evident in Figure 8.3, which graphically links bond rates to election outcomes. The figure shows that from 1952 through 1988 the victory or loss for the candidate of the incumbent president's party was correctly indicated by bond rates in all elections. When rates rose by at least **.58 percent** (58 basis points) over the two-year period from T-3 to T-1, the incumbent party candidate **lost**. Conversely, when rates dropped or rose no more than **.04 percent**, the incumbent candidate **won**. However, since 1988, this indicator has been less accurate. Between November 1989 and November 1991 bond rates dropped .48 percent, but President Bush nevertheless lost the 1992 election. Data for the 1996 and 2000 elections are in the inconclusive zone between the win and loss thresholds.

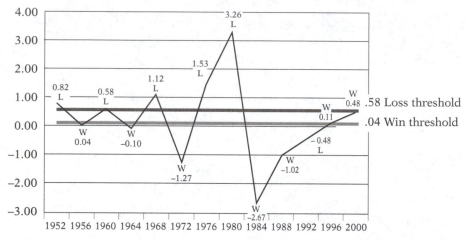

YIELD ON NEW HIGH-GRADE CORPORATE BONDS
Change from November Three Years Prior to 1 Year Prior to Election

W = Win for candidate of incumbent   L = Loss for candidate of incumbent
    president's party   president's party

1992 is misclassified
1996 and 2000 are inconclusive

Figure 8.3

DATA SOURCE: U.S. Federal Reserve (2000)

This interest rate indicator accounts for 47 percent of the variation in 1952–1996 election outcomes. Regressing the vote on this variable produces the following equation, which I use to forecast the 2000 election, after-the-fact. Bond rates increased .48 percent from November 1997 to November 1999 (T-1 to T-3), so that number is inserted into the equation to produce the 2000 forecast.

incumbent **(Gore)**
share of two-party = $53.2 - (2.851 \times \text{chg. bond rates}_{\text{Nov. 3 yrs. prior to Nov. 1 yr. prior}})$
vote in **2000**

$$= 53.2 - (2.851 \times .48)$$

$$= \textbf{51.8\%}$$

EQUATION 8.3

r^2 .47 (.42 adjusted)   Durbin-Watson score 2.242
t-value −2.997   standard error of estimate 4.753
    (significance .01)   number of elections 12 (1952–1996)

This forecast that the incumbent party candidate, Gore, would receive 51.8 percent of the two-party vote was only **1.5 percent in error** from the actual result, 50.3 percent. But the margin of error was large, +/−11.1 percent.

Long-Term Government Rates and Yield Spread

The second study using interest rates to forecast presidential elections is by Berry, Elliott, and Harpham (1996). In a simultaneous equations regression model, they found two interest rate variables linked to the vote: the average annual rate on 30-year government bonds, lagged one year behind the elections, and the difference ("spread") between this 30-year bond rate and the average annual rate on three-month treasury bills, both also lagged one year. (See Glossary for a description of lags.)

When I reproduced the data used by these analysts, none of the indicators was found to be significantly linked to the presidential vote. For the 1952–1992 period that they used, no variable accounted for more than 9 percent of the variation in election results (i.e., $r^2 = .09$). This result demonstrates the vast differences that can occur when variables are linked individually to election outcomes, compared to their use with other variables in multiple regressions. A comparison of this result with that in the previous section reveals that, at least when interest rate variables are considered separately, *change* in rates is more strongly related to presidential voting than are the actual rates.

Survey of Current Personal Finances

Since the 1940s, the Survey Research Center at the University of Michigan has conducted a national Survey of Consumers, quarterly in the early years and now monthly. (Tables of these results are available on the Web at **http://athena.sca.isr.umich.edu.**) In one question, interviewees are asked to assess their current financial situation, compared with the year earlier: "Would you say that you (and your family living there) are better off or worse off financially than you were a year ago?" (Survey Research Center 2001). Norpoth (1996) and Holbrook (1996a; 1996b) have found this retrospective assessment by the public to be strongly related to the vote for president. For 1952–1996, the correlation (r) between an index derived from surveys conducted in May of election years and the November presidential vote is an extraordinary .88. Squaring this figure means that **77 percent of the variation** in presidential election outcomes can be explained by consumers' perceptions of their personal financial situation five months before the election. However, when a regression was calculated, linking the vote for the incumbent party candidate with the May survey results, autocorrelation was found to be a significant problem. Since corrections for autocorrelation are beyond our purpose, regression of the vote on this variable was dropped. (Check the Glossary for a brief description of this problem.)

A line plot of the consumer financial survey data appears in Figure 8.4. The scale on the left side is the index of people's assessments of their current financial situation, compared to a year earlier. Higher values indicate more positive assessments. During the 1952–2000 period, with one exception, the candidate of the incumbent president's party **won** when these scores were **110 or higher** and **lost** when they were **108 or lower**. The misclassified year was 1968, when the incumbent party candidate, Democrat Hubert Humphrey, lost a close election even though the personal finance score was in the win category at 114.

CURRENT FINANCIAL SITUATION COMPARED TO YEAR EARLIER
Survey

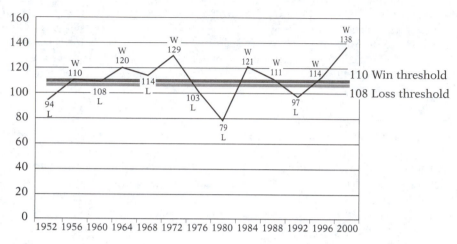

W = Win for candidate of incumbent   L = Loss for candidate of incumbent
      president's party   president's party

1968 is misclassified
2000 is popular vote "win"

Figure 8.4

DATA SOURCE: Survey Research Center (2001)

With 1952–1992 data, the 1996 election outcome would have been correctly predicted by this indicator, since the survey score for May 1996 was 114, above the win threshold of 110. The indicator's 138 reading in May 2000 was far higher than the win threshold. Indeed, Gore's close victory in the 2000 popular vote was hardly indicative of the strength of the survey indicator.

Stock Market Performance

In 1992, economist Richard Gleisner modified the well-known presidential forecasting model of Ray Fair by adding to it a measure of stock market performance, an approach also adopted by Haynes and Stone (1994). The indicator that Gleisner chose was the benchmark Dow Jones Industrial Average, specifically its rate of change from January to October of election years. It was assumed that a rising market is positive for the incumbent party candidate, whereas a falling market is negative. Over the 1908–1992 period used in the Haynes and Stone update (1994, 126), the correlation (r) between the Dow and the vote for president was .63, and the direction was positive as expected. Squaring this figure indicates that the Dow Jones average accounted for 40 percent of the variation in the presidential vote over this 84-year period. For 1952 through 1992, this figure drops to only 22 percent. A line plot had multiple misclassifications and thus is not reported.

Prospective Indicators

In this section, I turn to indicators that are measures of anticipated future economic conditions. The use of these variables assumes that voters make election choices on the basis of their assessments of the economy's likely performance in the future rather than in the past. Two of these indicators are derived from surveys of public opinion. The other is a multi-indicator index of various types of data.

Survey of Future Economic Conditions

The University of Michigan's Survey of Consumers, source of the previously described indicator of current personal finances, includes two other questions that have been used in forecasting efforts. Lockerbie (2000) chose a question in which respondents were asked to assess their financial prospects for the future rather than at present: "Now looking ahead—do you think that a year from now you (and your family living there) will be better off financially, or worse off, or just about the same as now?" (Survey Research Center 2001) Lockerbie used survey results for months in the second quarter of election years. These are available only from 1956 onward, thus creating a slightly shorter time series than for other variables that I have considered. A regression using these survey data explains 38 percent of variation in the vote from 1956 through 1996. A line plot had two misclassified elections.

The prospective question from this survey that Norpoth (1996) tested (though did not use in his final model) concerned people's views of future business conditions rather than their personal financial prospects: "Now turning to business conditions in the country as a whole—do you think that during the next 12 months we'll have good times financially, or bad times or what?" (Survey Research Center 2001) In a regression using 1952–1996 data, I have determined that this indicator can account for 28 percent of the variation in election outcomes, a somewhat weaker result than the question dealing with anticipated personal finances. A line plot has multiple misclassifications.

Index of Leading Economic Indicators

Each month, the Conference Board, a prominent business research organization, compiles an Index of Leading Economic Indicators. The index dates back to the 1930s and for many years, until late 1995, was a project of the BEA in the Department of Commerce. Since December 1996, the index has been comprised of ten quantitative indicators of economic activity, ranging from new building permits to stock market performance. It is designed to foretell the strength of the economy three to six months into the future and usually has been successful in doing so. If economic conditions influence the vote for president and if economic conditions can be anticipated that far into the future, this index could be a very useful election forecasting device that provides significant lead time.

Wlezien and Erikson (1996) have undertaken detailed analysis of the index and produced impressive results. Beginning with the first quarter of the respective presidents' terms, they calculated monthly change in the index and then summarized those results by quarter. A weighting scheme was employed similar to the one they and Hibbs applied to income, described previously. Each quarterly score was given a weight equal to 90 percent of the score for the following quarter, and the quarterly scores were then cumulated. Since the inverse of .9 is 1.11, each quarter's impact in the cumulative total was 1.11 times greater than that of the preceding quarter. In this way, recent quarters affect the total score somewhat more than early quarters.

Wlezien and Erikson tested the strength of association between election outcomes and the cumulative index values for various points throughout each president's term. They discovered that the strongest correlation (.85) was for data cumulated through 13 quarters, ending in March of the election year. Squaring this correlation figure reveals that the leading indicator index after 13 quarters can explain 72 percent of the variation in the vote for president in elections from 1952 through 1992, a very strong result for a single indicator.

I have attempted to replicate this promising approach with slight modifications. Data from 1961 through 1996 are of the current 10-indicator index and are available thanks to the Conference Board's work in recalculating the new index for those prior years (Conference Board 2000). The previous 11-indicator index was used for 1949 through 1960 (Darney 1996, 80). In calculating the cumulative index scores, I first totaled monthly changes in the index by quarter. Then each quarter's value was weighted so that it had 1.11 times the impact of the previous quarter's value. Finally, the weighted quarterly scores were summed and averaged.

To identify win-loss thresholds graphically, data for the 13-quarter cumulation of the leading indicators index are plotted in Figure 8.5. We see that the index is able to correctly classify the elections as wins or losses rather well. During the 1952–2000 period, in all elections but two (1968 and 1996), the candidate of the incumbent president's party **won** when the average quarterly index value was **.55 or higher**. Conversely, that candidate always **lost** when the index score dropped to **.32 or lower**. Those numbers thus define the win/loss thresholds. Unexpectedly, the 1996 index value, .15, is in the loss category. Thus, 1952–1992 data in the graph would have failed to correctly predict the reelection of President Clinton. The index's strong performance in 2000—.82—did correctly anticipate Gore's win in the popular vote, though, as we have seen with some other indicators, the relatively high score is not reflective of the closeness of the election.

Next, the index was correlated with election outcomes. My results, based on elections from 1952–1996, were similar to those of Erikson and Wlezien, though not quite as strong. The correlation of my 13-quarter index with the vote was .795, the square of which is .63. This means that the 13-quarter index of leading economic indicators is able to account for **63 percent of the variation** among election results from 1952 through 1996. Unfortunately, a regression of the vote on the 13-quarter index produced an equation with significant autocorrelation problems. As noted previously, corrections for autocorrelation are beyond the scope of this analysis. Thus, the regression is not reported, nor is it used to generate forecasts. (A description of autocorrelation is provided in the Glossary.)

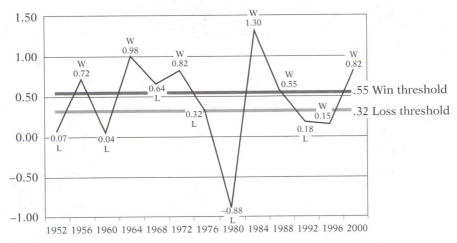

LEADING ECONOMIC INDICATORS
Quarterly Change, 13 Quarter Cumulation

W = Win for candidate of incumbent   L = Loss for candidate of incumbent
president's party   president's party

1968 and 1996 are misclassified
2000 is popular vote "win"

Figure 8.5

DATA SOURCES: Conference Board (2000)
                    Darnay (1996)

Another research team, Lewis-Beck and Tien (1996), also has used the Index of Leading Economic Indicators as a predictor of presidential election outcomes, though less successfully than Wlezien and Erikson. Lewis-Beck and Tien calculated change in the index over the first two quarters of election years. For any year in which the change was not consistently in the same direction for three months, that year was coded a zero. After exploring this indicator, they dropped it from their final 1996 forecasting model (Lewis-Beck and Tien 1996, 476).

Conclusion

The key findings in this chapter are summarized in Table 8.1. As evident in the table, one economic variable is individually able to account for more than three-fourths of the variation in election outcomes—consumers' assessments of their personal financial situations (77%). Not far behind is the Index of Leading Economic Indicators cumulated for 13 quarters (63%). Three other indicators can explain about half of the variation in election results: cumulative personal disposable income per capita (47%), second-quarter to second-quarter income growth (51%), and change in interest rates for long-term high-grade commercial bonds (47%).

Table 8.1 ECONOMIC INDICATORS SUMMARY

Indicator	% Variation in Vote Explained	1952–2000 Election Year Misclassified
Gross domestic product		
• 2nd quarter	38	1968
• first half	31	1968
Personal income		
• cumulative 14 quarters	47	1952
		1968
• 2nd quarter to 2nd quarter	51	1968
Interest rates		
• new high-grade corporate bonds (2-year change)	47	1992
Current personal finances		
• SRC survey	77	1968
Stock market performance		
• Dow-Jones average	22	multiple (pattern unclear)
Survey of future economic conditions		
• personal economic prospects	38	1956
		1960
• future business conditions	28	1960
		1976
		1988
		1992
Leading economic indicators		
• cumulative 13 quarters	63	1968
		1996

It is apparent that these variables have considerable explanatory power in accounting for election outcomes. But how well do they predict election results? In after-the-fact forecasts of the 2000 election, the indicators for which I reported regressions—the latter three—all were successful in identifying the election winner. However, the confidence intervals for these forecasts were large, revealing that the predictions of specific vote percentages lack a high degree of reliability. Significantly reducing the forecast confidence intervals will be possible only with equations having more than one variable. As we will see in the next chapter, which describes multi-variable models, some economic indicators are superb predictors of vote percentages in elections when used *in combination* with other variables.

But when economic indicators are used alone, the simpler forecasting technique of identifying win and loss thresholds in line plots is likely preferable. With the latter approach, we found that line plots for four of the economic indicators correctly classified elections from 1952 through 1996 as wins or losses, with only one exception for each. On the basis of these patterns observed for that period, the 2000 election was correctly predicted by second-quarter GDP growth, income growth from mid-year to mid-year, the survey of current personal finances, and the Index of Leading Economic Indicators. Apart from the misclassification of 1996 by the latter indicator, results were similar in predicting the 1996 election from the graphs.

Appendix 8.1
Equations for 2004
Election Scenarios

Unlike in some other chapters, projected scenarios for the 2004 election are not presented for the single economic indicators for which equations were generated to predict the 2000 election. With confidence intervals for the 2000 forecasts exceeding $+/-10$ percent, a scenario exercise for 2004 seems problematic. However, for the reader's information, in this appendix I present the equations, updated through the 2000 election, which could be used for scenarios in 2004. The Republican candidate is considered to be the incumbent party candidate in that year, given the assumption that the election is a referendum on the sitting president's stewardship of the economy.

Income Growth—Cumulative 14 Quarters

incumbent (**Rep.**)
share of two-party $= 45.434 + (1.073 \times$ cumulative income growth$_{14\ quarters})$
vote in **2004**

r^2 .47 (.42 adjusted)	Durbin-Watson score 2.276
t-value 3.132	standard error of estimate 4.569
(significance .01)	number of elections 13 (1952–2000)

Income Growth—2nd Quarter Prior Year to 2nd Quarter Election Year

incumbent (**Rep.**)
share of two-party $= 48.313 + (1.917 \times$ income growth$_{mid-year\ to\ mid-year})$
vote in **2004**

r^2 .50 (.45 adjusted)	Durbin-Watson score 2.824
t-value 3.313	standard error of estimate 4.447
(significance .01)	number of elections 13 (1952-2000)

Bond Rates—Change from November Three Years Prior to November One Year Prior to Election

incumbent (**Rep.**)
share of two-party $= 53.082 - (2.870 \times$ chg. bond rates$_{Nov.\ 3\ yrs.\ prior\ to\ Nov.\ 1\ yr.\ prior})$
vote in **2004**

r^2 .48 (.43 adjusted)	Durbin-Watson score 2.262
t-value -3.153	standard error of estimate 4.555
(significance .01)	number of elections 13 (1952–2000)

9
★ ★ ★

Putting It All Together: Multivariate Forecasting Models

A good model has predictive value.
That about sums it up.

Professor Grierson
in John Kenneth Galbraith,
A Tenured Professor: A Novel

In previous chapters, I have assessed the ability of single indicators to fore-cast the outcome of presidential elections. In this chapter, the focus shifts to *combinations* of indicators to determine the extent to which, taken together, they can provide better predictions than can indicators used alone. Indeed, nearly all forecasting models of presidential elections have included multiple indicators, because normally they have greater explanatory power and fore-casting accuracy than do single-variable equations.

Most of these multiple-variable ("multivariate") models compare influences on elections existing at the national level with national election results, for 10 to 13 post–World War II election years. They thus use election years as the unit of analysis, as do most single-indicator models described in previous chapters. But in this approach, the objective is to link the vote in election years with *multiple* influences preceding the elections that can explain that vote. To predict an upcoming election, one determines current values for indicators reflecting these national-level influences and inserts these data into the multivariate equa-tion that represents the historical pattern between the indicators and the vote.

In contrast to national election year models, a few studies focus on state elec-tion results and factors common to all states that influence the state outcomes. These "pooled time series" models include data for all (or most) states for sev-eral elections within one equation. Forecasts of the national vote are made by predicting election outcomes in each state, then predicting the number of peo-ple likely to vote in each state, merging these voting and turnout estimates by state, and finally combining the results for all included states.

In this chapter, I first look at various national level models. Next is a description of two pooled state models, which are more complex and offer greater diversity of influences. Finally, I demonstrate the use of hypothetical scenarios in which forecasts are made of possible election results, contingent on specified assumptions.

National Level Models

The work of most presidential election forecasters has focused on comparing national influences on elections with results of the national vote for a given number of election years. Forecasting models of this type have used several different combinations of indicators: those that rely primarily on multiple measures of economic performance and those that combine indicators of economic growth with presidential approval ratings, with tenure in office, with trial heat polls, with congressional elections, or with prior voting patterns in presidential elections.

Economic Performance

It was in 1978 that the first multivariate regression models to forecast presidential elections appeared. Several were created by economist Ray Fair of Yale University. Fair's Yale colleague, political scientist Edward Tufte, also developed a prototype (1978). Fair's objective was to demonstrate the impact of national economic conditions on presidential elections, leading him to emphasize multiple economic indicators. (As described in Chapter 8, the underlying assumption is that voters view the president as being responsible for the state of the economy and reward or punish the candidate of the president's party accordingly.)

Tufte used both political and economic variables, including a survey index of interviewees' net likes and dislikes of presidential candidates, as well as annual change in real disposable income per capita. Because Tufte's data from the American National Election Studies were not available until after the election, his work was not a true forecasting model. Of the two scholars, Fair has remained active in election forecasting, while Tufte has largely moved on to other interests. Both, however, have exerted considerable influence on election forecasters within their respective disciplines.

Fair's Pre-1996 Models

Fair's first article (1978) on presidential election forecasting described several equations using different combinations of indicators including economic growth, inflation, unemployment, military strength, and incumbency. It was not until his next article (1982) that Fair stated a clear preference for one version, the first model reported in Table 9.1 and summarized later in this section. He continued to apply this equation to successive elections until revising it for 1996.

Fair's models have included longer time spans than have many others, generally from 1916 onward. These equations have the statistical advantage of

Table 9.1 THE FAIR FAMILY OF MODELS

	Fair 1992 Model (1996a, 92)	Gleisner 1992 Model (1992, 388)	Haynes-Stone 1992 Model (1994, 127)	Fair 1996 Model (1996a, 96)
GNP/GDP per cap (× Inc. party)	.0104 (5.30)	.0060 (5.63)	.017 (2.72)	.0065 (8.03)
GNP/GDP deflator (× Inc. party)	−.0031 (−1.07)	−.0046 (−3.30)	−.030 (−2.48)	−.0083 (−3.40)
Incumbent pres.	.0424 (2.74)	.0516 (5.51)		.052 (4.58)
Incumbent party	.0053 (0.34)		.458 (4.44)	−.034 (−1.26)
Time trend	.0036 (1.97)			
"Good news" (× Inc. party)				.0099 (4.46)
Terms in office (× GNP/GDP deflator)			−.148 (3.72)	−.024 (−2.23)
War years (× Inc. party)				.047 (2.09)
Dow-Jones (× Inc. party)		.0018 (5.25)	.415 (1.99)	
Military/pop			.013 (2.43)	
Military/pop (× GNP/GDP per cap)			−.100 (−3.18)	
Military/pop (× GNP/GDP deflator)			−.223 (−2.56)	
Constant	.4021 (11.70)	.4667 (19.31)	−.098 (−2.43)	.468 (90.62)
Number elections	19 (1916–88)	21 (1908–88)	22 (1908–92)	20 (1916–92)
R^2	.89	.89 (adj.)	.89	.96
Standard error	.0296	.0245	.125	.0190
Durbin-Watson	—	2.309	1.977	—

t-values are in parentheses.
Some values reported in sources have been rounded off.
Dependent variable: Democratic candidate's share of two-party vote.
All variables in Haynes-Stone model are significant at .05 level. Significance values are not reported for variables in sources for other models.
Missing values for equation characteristics denote unreported data in source and are indicated by a dash.

being derived from a larger number of cases than the more common post–World War II models of most political scientists. However, fitting the data to election outcomes is more difficult, because greater diversity exists among the elections and attendant socioeconomic conditions since 1916, compared with these phenomena since World War II.

Fair's indicator for the election result differs from that in most political scientists' forecasting models. He seeks to predict the share of the two-party vote for the **Democratic candidate** rather than that for the candidate of the incumbent president's party. In order to account for the impact of incumbency, he creates a dummy variable in which elections with a Democratic incumbent are coded "1" and those with a Republican incumbent are coded "−1". Economic indicators are then multiplied by this incumbent party indicator, creating interactive variables. Thus, when economic conditions are good and the president is a Democrat, that is expected to enhance the vote for the Democratic candidate, with the reverse effect when the president is a Republican. Poor economic performance is accounted for in similar fashion.

The indicators in Fair's equations through the 1992 election are:

- **Economic growth:** Growth rate in real per capita gross national product (GNP) in the second and third quarters of the election year (multiplied by −1 if the incumbent party is Republican)
- **Inflation:** Growth rate in GNP deflator in the two-year period before the election (multiplied by −1 if the incumbent party is Republican)
- **Presidential incumbency:** Dummy variable indicating whether the sitting President is running for reelection (+1 if incumbent is a Democrat; −1 if incumbent is a Republican; zero if no incumbent)
- **Party incumbency:** Dummy variable for the party of the incumbent President (+1 if a Democrat; −1 if a Republican)
- **Time trend:** Sequential numbers for each successive election; believed by Fair to favor Democratic candidates

Using an equation based on these indicators (reported in the first column of Table 9.1), Fair gained notoriety by correctly forecasting Reagan's victories in 1980 and 1984, and Bush's win in 1988 (though he noted that the latter was in fact too close to call). However, Fair's prediction of a Bush victory over Clinton in 1992 was far off the mark (1996b). His assumptions as to values for variables in the third quarter varied somewhat during the campaign, producing slightly different forecasts. In all of these predictions, however, Bush was consistently picked to be the winner by Fair. In early August, for example, he forecast that Bush would receive 57 percent of the two-party vote, when in fact Bush garnered only 46.5 percent (Pennar 1992).

Fair's 1996 Model

The missteps in 1992, which were well publicized, led Fair to revise his model substantially for the 1996 election. In the 1996 version, Fair made several changes—adding three variables, modifying two, retaining two unchanged, and dropping one (the time trend) (Fair 1996a).

Fair's *new* variables included:

- **"Good news":** Number of quarters, from among the first 15 quarters of the president's term, in which GDP per capita grew at an annual rate of 2.9 percent or more (positive in equation)

- **Duration of president's party in office:** "0" if incumbent party has been in office for one or two terms, "1" for Democrats and "−1" for Republicans for three terms, "1.25" for Democrats and "−1.25" for Republicans for four terms, and so on (negative in equation)

- **War years adjustment:** inflation and "good news" in 1920, 1944, and 1948 are coded "0"

His *modified* variables included:

- **Economic growth:** For first three quarters rather than only second and third quarters; measured by change in GDP rather than GNP (positive in equation)

- **Inflation:** For first 15 quarters of president's term rather than the two-year period before the election; measured by the deflator for GDP rather than that for GNP (negative in equation)

His *unchanged* variables (both described previously) included:

- **Presidential incumbency**
- **Party incumbency**

    As evident in Table 9.1, last column, this 1996 model of Fair's accounted for 96 percent of the variation among results of the presidential elections in the historical data set, compared with 89 percent in the 1992 model. Further slight adjustments later appeared in the equation (Fair 1998).

    As early as the first of January 1996, Fair announced forecasts produced by his new model ("It's Predictable" 1996; Passell 1996). His forecasts necessarily incorporated economic projections through the third quarter of 1996 because three of his five independent variables required data through that period. At that time, his model predicted a narrow Clinton defeat with 49 percent of the two-party vote. A forecast published by Fair in the summer of 1996 was essentially the same, putting Clinton's vote at 49.5 percent (Fair 1996a, 100). *After the election*, using actual data for the third quarter variables, Fair reported that the equation estimated a Clinton victory with 51.4 percent of the two-party vote. This represented a 3.3 percent forecast error, given Clinton's 1996 vote share of 54.7 percent.

    If Fair's 1996 forecasts suffered from variations in estimated values of his causal variables, his predictions in 2000 demonstrated the benefit of consistent, accurate long-term estimates. Using an updated version of his 1996 model, on April 2, 2000, Fair posted a prediction on his Web site that Gore would receive 50.8 percent of the two-party vote (**http://fairmodel.econ. yale.edu/vote/vot1198.htm**). He forecast the same margin for Gore again on July 31, 2000, and finally on October 27, 2000, a few days before the election.

The actual data for Fair's causal variables had become available in time for the last forecast and were virtually identical to the earlier estimates produced by his econometric model of the U.S. economy (Fair 2000).

Fair's predictions of the 2000 election were closer to the outcome than those of any other multivariate model that we have considered. Since Gore received 50.3 percent of the two-party vote, his 50.8 percent prediction was only 0.5 percent in error.

Adding Stock Market Performance

Fair's seminal work became a catalyst underlying other applications of multivariate techniques to forecasting presidential elections from economic data. Some researchers piggy-backed directly on Fair's model, attempting improvements in it. One was Richard Gleisner (1992), an economist at St. Cloud State University in Minnesota. Like Fair, Gleisner included economic growth, inflation, and an indicator of whether the president was running for reelection. However, Gleisner's equation added stock market performance as measured by the **Dow-Jones Industrial Average**, January through October of the election year. Two of Fair's indicators were dropped: time trend and party incumbency.

Gleisner's equation, seen in Table 9.1, seems to fit the data well, accounting for 89 percent of variation in the vote. However, the model provides only one-month lead time, and its credibility has suffered from weak forecasting performance. In a 1992 journal article, the Gleisner model predicted that Bush would receive 58 percent of the two-party vote, an error of more than 11 percent from the election result (1992, 390). Updates later in the campaign season evidently were not published.

Adding Military, Incumbent Terms in Office

Another revision of Fair's model was undertaken by Stephen Haynes and Joe Stone (1994), both economists at the University of Oregon. Their equation included three of Fair's indicators—economic growth, inflation, and party of the incumbent president—along with Gleisner's stock market variable. In addition, Haynes and Stone used two variables that incorporated a political dimension beyond Fair's incumbency indicator. Like the Fair and Gleisner equations, the Haynes and Stone model accounted for 89 percent of the variation in the outcome of previous elections in the data set.

One of the additional political indicators was a military variable, change in the proportion of the **population in the armed forces** for the two years prior to the election. Haynes and Stone included this indicator separately and also treated it interactively in combination with economic growth and with inflation. The separate relationship of the military variable to the vote was positive, presumably because threats to national security (evident in growth of the armed forces) increase support for the incumbent president—a rally-around-the-flag effect (1994, 128).

Haynes and Stone also used a dummy variable for **number of terms** that the incumbent party has occupied the White House, interacting with inflation. The combined indicator penalizes a party for retaining the presidency a long time when the economy is performing poorly—somewhat akin to Abramowitz's two-term penalty. Two of Fair's original variables were dropped: time trend and the dummy variable denoting an incumbent president running for reelection. (See Table 9.1.) According to Haynes and Stone, for 1992 their model would have incorrectly predicted a very narrow loss for Clinton with 49.7 percent of the two-party vote. The actual Clinton vote, 53.5 percent, was outside the 3.4 percent forecast confidence interval, though only slightly (1994, 127).

Presidential Approval and the Economy

While academic economists were developing the Fair family of models, and business economists were creating other election models based on economic indicators (Koretz 1992), several political scientists were following the tradition of Tufte by creating models that emphasized both economic and political influences. The first published was in 1984 by Michael Lewis-Beck and Tom Rice of the University of Iowa and the University of Vermont, respectively. (See Table 9.2.) Their work introduced presidential approval ratings into the same model with economic indicators, a combination that other researchers have used as well. As explained in Chapter 3, the role of presidential approval ratings in forecasting elections for president is based on the assumption that these elections are in part a voter referendum on the job performance of the sitting president, which may work to the benefit or detriment of the candidate of the president's party. As I also have noted, measures of economic performance function much the same way in the narrower economic domain.

Approval Ratings and GNP Growth

The economic variable chosen by Lewis-Beck and Rice (1984) in this early effort was growth of the economy, measured by change in **gross national product (GDP) per capita**. Fair had used this indicator, too, but Lewis-Beck and Rice limited it to the **second quarter** of the election year. To this they added **presidential approval ratings for May** of that year, building on the work of Brody and Sigelman, who the previous year (1983) had used approval ratings prior to the election to forecast the 1984 election result (discussed in Chapter 3).

In combining these economic and political variables into one model, Lewis-Beck and Rice strengthened the previous efforts by Fair and by Brody and Sigelman. The addition of a political dimension overcame Fair's dependence on economic influences. Adding GNP to presidential approval ratings broadened the Brody and Sigelman model, increasing its explanatory power. However, the Lewis-Beck and Rice equation included only nine elections (1948–1980) and accounted for 82 percent of the variation in election results. Lewis-Beck and Rice calculated conditional forecasts for their model, given that values for the independent variables were unavailable at the time of publication. Each of these scenarios correctly foresaw a Reagan victory in 1984, although the forecast confidence intervals were likely large.

Adding a Two-Term Penalty

The next multivariate model building effort based on presidential approval ratings was by political scientist Alan Abramowitz of Emory University and is reported in Table 9.2 (1988, 847, Note 3). Drawing on Lewis-Beck and Rice, this equation included **approval ratings** and **GNP growth during the first half** of the election year. Abramowitz's innovation was the addition of a dummy variable to specify whether the incumbent president's party had occupied the White House for the **two previous terms**. His assumption was that voters are inclined to change parties in the White House after two consecutive terms, but not after one term. This variable was in effect a two-term penalty—and one-term reward—indicator. (See Chapter 6.)

By adding the two-term dummy variable, Abramowitz was able to explain an additional 10 percent of variation in the vote beyond what Lewis-Beck and Rice had explained when using only presidential approval ratings and GNP growth. The adjusted R^2 for the ten-election equation (1948–1984) was thereby raised to an impressive .92. No other forecasting model up to that time had accounted for as much as 92 percent of the variation in presidential election outcomes. No forecast was attempted with this model for the 1988 election, although Abramowitz used a similar model to generate conditional forecast scenarios. Using preliminary data in the latter equation, Abramowitz forecast a Bush victory over Dukakis with 51.2 percent of the two-party vote, 2.7 percent off of the actual Bush vote (53.9%) (1988, 846). The forecast confidence interval was not reported, however, nor was the standard error of the estimate needed to calculate it.

Adding Primaries and House Seats

In their 1992 book, *Forecasting Elections*, Lewis-Beck and Rice published a modified version of their 1984 model. (See Table 9.2.) Rather than forecasting the incumbent's popular vote, as before, they now sought to predict the share of the *electoral* vote going to the incumbent party candidate. As to predictor variables, they continued to use **presidential approval ratings**, though for **July** rather than for May as in their earlier effort. Lewis-Beck and Rice also retained **GNP growth**, opting for data from the **first half of the election year** rather than the second quarter in their previous model. To these they added two other variables: vote received by the incumbent party's candidate in the **presidential primary elections** (dummy variable: "1" = 60% of the vote or more; "0" = less than 60%); and the number of seats lost (or won) by the incumbent president's party in the House of Representatives in **mid-term elections** two years earlier. Although this model accounted for 92 percent of variation in the vote for the 11 elections from 1948 through 1988, it failed to correctly predict the winner of the 1992 election. With perhaps one exception, neither this approach nor others that were first used for predicting the 1992 election appear among the prominent forecasting models today. Some predate 1992; the origin of most others is 1996. (Other 1992 models appear at **http://web.polmeth.ufl.edu/tpm/TPMV5N2.pdf.**)

Table 9.2 Presidential Approval and the Economy

	Lewis-Beck and Rice (1984, 17)	Lewis-Beck and Rice (1992, 52)	Lewis-Beck and Tien (1996, 477)	Abramowitz (1988, 847)	Abramowitz (1996, 438)	Wlezien and Erikson (1996, 496)	Wlezien and Erikson (1996, 501)	Holbrook (1996b, 512)
Presidential approval	.34 (4.05)	.86** (3.39)	.16** (2.11)	.18 (3.6)	.208*** (4.74)	.30** (4.25)	.22** (2.87)	.088** (2.06)
GNP/GDP	1.42 (1.78)	7.76** (3.79)	1.83** (3.33)	1.9 (5.1)	.773*** (4.07)			
Cum. income						7.35** (2.49)		
Peace and prosperity			.14** (2.35)					
Cum. leading econ. indicators							28.37*** (3.38)	
Mid-term House seat loss		.52** (2.87)						
Personal finances								.304** (8.12)
Incumbent share of total primary vote	19.66** (3.30)							

Two-term penalty				-5.3 (-3.9)	-4.416^{***} (-3.84)			-4.549^{**} (-4.74)
Constant	33.03	6.83 (0.50)	27.34 (6.11)	42.8	42.544	33.97*** (10.52)	39.06*** (10.69)	17.796** (5.09)
R^2	.82	.95	.92	—	—	—	—	.965
Adjusted R^2	—	.92	.88	.92	.923	.80	.83	.952
Standard error of estimate	3.68	9.10	2.26	—	1.728	2.88	2.69	1.36
Durbin-Watson	—	2.34	1.87	—	—	—	—	—
Number of elections	9 (1948–80)	11 (1948–88)	11 (1952–92)	10 (1948–84)	12 (1948–92)	11 (1952–92)	11 (1952–92)	12 (1948–92)

*** sig. .01
** sig. .05
* sig. .10
t-values are in parentheses.
Significance values are not reported in Lewis-Beck and Rice (1984) and Abramowitz (1988) for variables in those models.
Missing values for equation characteristics denote unreported data in source and are indicated by a dash.
Dependent variable: share of two-party popular vote received by candidate of incumbent president's party (electoral vote used in Lewis-Beck and Rice 1992).

1996 Models and Updates with 1996, 2000 Forecasts: Approval Ratings and the Economy

When the American Political Science Association (APSA) met in early fall 1996, two months before the presidential election, political science election fore-casters were ready. Several models were presented along with predictions derived from them. Most of the models continued the prior emphasis on pres-idential approval ratings and economic indicators. The papers describing these efforts were published later that fall in a special issue of the *American Politics Quarterly*. That issue of the journal, in turn, was updated and expanded to pro-vide conditional forecasts of the 2000 election and published as a book enti-tled *Before the Vote: Forecasting American National Elections* (Campbell and Garand 2000).

The 1996 APSA models were well-crafted. Most explained more than 90 percent of the variation in the historical election results and had narrow fore-cast confidence intervals. Key statistical characteristics, including standard errors and autocorrelation test results, were reported, in contrast to articles describing some earlier models. In short, these papers projected the image of a field of study that appeared to be coming of age. All presenters on the APSA panel made forecasts of the 1996 election outcome at the meeting (or shortly afterward), and, as seen in the descriptions in this section, all forecasts cor-rectly predicted a Clinton victory.

Updated versions of most of the 1996 models were presented at the 2000 meeting of the APSA on August 31. All forecast a Gore victory, with two-party vote shares ranging from 52.8 to 60.3 percent. The average of these predic-tions (as later corrected) was 56.0 percent for Gore, compared to the 50.3 per-cent that he actually received. The performance of the models in 2000 is reported in the following sections, along with the 1996 results.

Approval Ratings, GNP, Peace and Prosperity.   In developing a forecasting model for 1996, Lewis-Beck had a new collaborator, Charles Tien, then a graduate student working with him at the University of Iowa (now on the faculty at Hunter College, CUNY). As in Lewis-Beck's 1992 effort with Tom Rice, this model again included **July presidential approval ratings** and **first half GNP growth**, but it also added a new variable.

The latter was a **peace and prosperity** survey indicator, created from responses to two Gallup Poll questions assessing public expectations of the major parties' likely performance in these two areas. As to peace, this survey question was used: "Looking ahead for the next few years, which political party do you think would be more likely to keep the United States out of war—the Republican or the Democratic party?" Expectations of party performance in promoting prosperity were determined by responses to this question: "Which political party—the Republican or the Democratic—will do a better job of keeping the country prosperous" (Lewis-Beck and Tien 1996, 474)? By requiring voters to project into the future, this indicator captures prospective influences on voting. In contrast, the economic growth and presidential approval variables assume that voters look to past performance of the economy and of the president. Thus, the distinguishing characteristic of the Lewis-Beck and Tien model is its introduction of both retrospective and prospective influences on voting into election forecasting.

Although the peace and prosperity indicator is a significant influence in the model, as are the other two, its validity could be questioned because not all of the surveys that comprise it were conducted in the same month of election years. Survey months for most years were from May to August, although January and October surveys were included, as well (Lewis-Beck and Tien 1996, 489). Yet the model is strong, accounting for 92 percent of the variation among election results in the data set. (See Table 9.2.) Using data from 1952–1992, it forecast Clinton to be the 1996 election winner with 54.8 percent of the two-party vote, an error of only 0.1 percent. The election result obviously is well within the 95 percent forecast confidence interval (1996, 533). The prediction was made two months before the election; data estimates in fact were available a month prior to that.

When Lewis-Beck and Tien updated their model for the 2000 election, new values for the same indicators predicted a Gore victory with 55.4 percent of the two-party vote. This forecast, made on August 25 shortly before the APSA meeting, was 5.1 percent too high, given Gore's 50.3 percent share of the two-party vote ("Forecasts" 2000).

Approval Ratings, GDP, Two-Term Penalty. The 1996 version of Abramowitz's model was similar to that of 1988. It included **early July approval ratings**, **GDP growth for the first half** of the election year, and the **two-term penalty** dummy ("1" = president's party in White House eight or more years; "0" = four years). As evident in Table 9.2, this 1948–1992 equation was strong, accounting for 92 percent of the variation in the historical vote on an adjusted basis. Its prediction that Clinton would receive 56.8 percent of the 1996 two-party vote was 2.1 percent in error, given Clinton's vote share of 54.7 percent. The Abramowitz forecast was made on August 5, 1996, shortly after the economic data became available (1996, 532).

For the 2000 election the updated Abramowitz model predicted that Gore would receive 53.2 percent of the two-party vote. This forecast, made on August 1, was 2.9 percent higher than Gore's actual share of the vote, 50.3 percent ("Forecasts" 2000).

Approval Ratings, Income, Leading Economic Indicators. Robert Erikson and Christopher Wlezien produced several equations in 1996. Both professors were then on the faculty at the University of Houston, although Erikson has since moved to Columbia University. One group, first published in March, included two variables: **presidential approval ratings** and **cumulative personal income** (Erikson and Wlezien 1996). The latter indicator followed Hibbs's cumulative approach to income measurement described in Chapter 8.

Using data from 1952 through 1992, Erikson and Wlezien calculated separate equations that included the income index cumulated for progressively longer periods of time, together with average presidential approval ratings for a recent quarter. These explorations were insightful, though the pre-election equations were not strong. For example, the equation that included income cumulated for 14 quarters and presidential approval ratings for the 14th quarter (ending June 30) accounted for 67 percent of the variation in the vote on an adjusted basis. For the 15-quarter model, ending September 30, this figure is 80 percent. (The latter equation is reported in Table 9.2.)

In their primary 1996 effort presented at the fall APSA meeting, Wlezien and Erikson (1996) tested several combinations of variables, which included cumulative income and approval ratings. To forecast the 1996 election, they settled on a model that included average **presidential approval ratings** for the **14th quarter** (April through June) and the **Index of Leading Economic Indicators** cumulated for **quarters 1 through 13** of the president's term. (See Chapters 3 and 8 for a description of the indicators and Table 9.2 for the equation.) This equation explained 83 percent of the variation in past election outcomes. It correctly forecast the 1996 winner, predicting 54.5 percent for Clinton, with a remarkably low forecast error of only 0.2 percent. The probability of a Clinton victory was 89 percent. (An amended later forecast was less accurate [1996, 534]).

At the fall 2000 APSA meeting, Wlezien and Erikson presented a slightly altered version of their 1996 model. As we have seen, the earlier model included presidential approval ratings for the 14th quarter of the president's term—that is, the second quarter of the election year. For 2000, however, Wlezien and Erikson used approval ratings for the 15th quarter, July through September. Since their forecast was made on August 25, an estimate of future ratings through September was necessary. For the Index of Leading Economic Indicators, cumulated values through the 13th quarter continued to be used in 2000. With a model incorporating these variables, Wlezien and Erikson predicted that Gore would receive 55.2 percent of the two-party vote, which was 4.9 percent in error, given Gore's 50.3 percent vote share ("Forecasts" 2000).

Approval Ratings, Consumer Attitudes, Two-Term Penalty.   Another model using presidential approval ratings was presented at the 1996 APSA meeting by Thomas Holbrook of the University of Wisconsin, Milwaukee (1996a, 25–28; 1996b). As Lewis-Beck and Tien had done, Holbrook included survey results as a variable. He used a question from the University of Michigan's Survey of Consumers described in Chapter 8: "Would you say that you (and your family living there) are better off or worse off financially than you were a year ago?" Specifically, the indicators in Holbrook's model were average **presidential approval ratings in the second quarter**, retrospective **personal financial assessments** from responses to the preceding survey question in **May** of election years, and the incumbent party **two-term penalty** indicator used by Abramowitz. The resulting equation accounted for 95.2 percent of the variation in the historical 1948–1992 vote, as adjusted. (See Table 9.2.) For the 1996 election, the model predicted that Clinton would receive 57.2 percent of the two-party vote, which was off 2.5 percent from Clinton's actual vote, 54.7 percent. The election result was within the 95 percent forecast confidence interval of +/−3.5 percent.

Updating his 1996 model, Holbrook produced a forecast of the 2000 election in early July. His prediction was far off the mark—10 percent too high. He estimated that Gore would receive 60.3 percent of the two-party vote, when in fact Gore garnered only 50.3 percent. Holbrook's model reflected both the extraordinarily high level of consumer confidence recorded in May 2000, by the Survey of Consumers and President Clinton's impressive approval ratings in the second quarter, which averaged 58.3 percent ("Forecasts" 2000).

Years in Office and the Economy

Brad Lockerbie of the University of Georgia also presented a forecasting model at the 1996 APSA meeting. However, it was not published in the *American Politics Quarterly* that year with the work of the other presenters, though it did appear with their papers later reprinted in *Before the Vote* (Lockerbie 2000). As described in Chapter 6, Lockerbie devised an indicator based on the number of consecutive **years that the incumbent president's party had occupied the White House**. Much of the rationale underlying this indicator is similar to that for Abramowitz's two-term penalty indicator.

Lockerbie also included two economic variables, described in Chapter 8. One was change in **per capita real disposable income** from the second quarter of the year before the election to the second quarter of the election year (i.e., mid-year to mid-year). This, of course, is a retrospective indicator, reflecting economic conditions in the recent past. Lockerbie's second economic indicator was prospective, assessing the public's view of their **personal economic prospects** in the future. A question from the University of Michigan's Survey of Consumers provided the data: "Now looking ahead—do you think that a year from now you (and your family living there) will be better off financially, or worse off, or just about the same as now?" (By focusing on the future, this survey indicator is similar to the Gallup Poll's question on the outlook for prosperity used in Lewis-Beck and Tien's peace and prosperity variable, described previously.) In short, Lockerbie assumes that voters are influenced both by past economic conditions and by anticipated future economic conditions. When voters are satisfied with the state of the economy—experienced in the past and anticipated in the future—they will tend to retain the party of the incumbent president in the White House. If not, they will vote for a change.

Lockerbie's equation is reported in Table 9.3, right column. Using data for the ten election years from 1956 through 1992, the equation accounted for 96 percent of the variation in the vote received by the incumbent party candidate. For 1996, it forecast a Clinton victory with 57.56 percent of the two-party vote, a forecast error of 2.9 percent. Lockerbie put the probability of Clinton winning at 99 percent.

Lockerbie's forecast of the 2000 election was made from a slightly altered update of his 1996 model. As noted previously, the earlier version included a measure of change in income from the middle of the year before the election to the middle of the election year. In the revised model, this income growth indicator covered the calendar year prior to the election. For 2000 Lockerbie predicted a Gore victory with 60.3 percent of the two-party vote. Since Gore in fact received only 50.3 percent of the vote, Lockerbie's forecast error was a

Table 9.3 VARIED ECONOMIC MODELS

	Lewis-Beck (1985, 58)	Campbell (1996, 416)	Alesina et al. (1996, 123)	Norpoth (1996, 457)	Lockerbie (2000, 137)
Trial heat poll	.52 (7.77)	.56*** (10.60)			
GNP/GDP	1.42 (3.08)	2.08*** (5.14)	1.46 (4.75)	.32 (1.36)	
Income					.68 (1.49)
Vote for House, mid-term			2.01 (3.30)		
Seat share in House			−.78 (−2.81)		
Inflation				−.74** (−2.55)	
Candidates' primary strength				3.43** (2.64)	
Vote (4 years earlier)				.41*** (2.96)	
Vote (8 years earlier)				−.35** (−2.65)	

	(1948–80)	(1948–92)	(1916–92)	(1912–92)	(1956–92)
Future personal finances					1.10 (5.81)
Years in office					−22.08 (−8.11)
Constant	26.84	22.69	−12.39 (−.65)	—	30.72
R^2	.94	—	.61	—	.96
Adjusted R^2	—	.939	—	.77	—
Standard error of estimate	2.15	1.49	—	1.50	—
Durbin-Watson	—	—	—	—	2.18
Number of elections	9	12	20	21	10

*** sig. .01
** sig. .05
t-values are in parentheses.
Unreported equation characteristics denoted by a dash.
Significance values for variables in Lewis-Beck (1985) and Lockerbie (2000) models are not reported in sources, though in fact all are significant at the .05 level or higher except for Lockerbie's income indicator.
Dependent variable: share of two-party vote received by candidate of incumbent president's party.

very large 10 percent. (This forecast is a corrected version of the one presented at the 2000 APSA meeting [Lockerbie 2001].)

Trial Heat Polls and the Economy

Trial heat public opinion polls during a presidential campaign, pitting party nominees against one another, provide a measure of the relative strength of both candidates, not merely support for the incumbent party candidate reflected in economic indicators and presidential approval ratings. We saw in Chapter 1 that trial heats, used alone, have been able to explain a high percentage of the vote historically. Can the explanatory power of these polls used singly be improved by adding an economic variable, as was found to be true with presidential approval ratings?

In 1985, Michael Lewis-Beck became the first researcher to use both trial heat polls and a measure of economic conditions in one equation. He thus pioneered this use of trial heats only a year after he and Tom Rice had led the way in including both presidential approval ratings and economic growth in a single regression. As he and Rice had done with approval ratings, Lewis-Beck combined trial heats with **per capita GNP growth for the second quarter** of the election year. Using **trial heats** at the onset of the fall campaign in **early September**, together with GNP growth, he produced an equation that explained 94 percent of variation in the historical vote. This impressive result, reported in Table 9.3, is especially noteworthy for an equation based on only nine elections (1948–1980).

Five years later a similar equation was produced by James Campbell, then of Louisiana State University (now of the University at Buffalo, SUNY) and Kenneth Wink, at that time a graduate student at LSU (now on the faculty at Western Carolina University). After changing Lewis-Beck's economic variable slightly, eliminating the per capita adjustment to second quarter GNP growth, Campbell and Wink (1990) computed successive regressions, varying trial heats at intervals from June to November. The best forecasting equation paired early September trial heats with GNP growth, which thereby confirmed Lewis-Beck's earlier findings. Although Lewis-Beck did not pursue trial heats, instead favoring models based on presidential approval ratings, Campbell continued with this approach. His 1996 model, presented at the APSA meeting early that fall, combined trial heats with economic growth in the second quarter, as in the past. The only slight change from his earlier effort with Wink was in the economic growth variable, in substituting second quarter gross *domestic* product for second quarter gross *national* product. Campbell's equation continued to be strong, again accounting for 94 percent of the variation in election outcomes in the 1948–1992 data set (1996, 416). (See this model in Table 9.3, second column.)

Campbell's forecast for 1996 was made on September 5, 1996, two months before the election. He predicted that Clinton would receive 58.11 percent of the two-party vote, a forecast that was 3.4 percent in error, given that Clinton garnered 54.7 percent. Based on this equation, Campbell estimated a 96 percent probability of Clinton winning (1996, 533).

Campbell's update of his earlier model for the 2000 election resulted in a forecast of 52.8 percent of the two-party vote for Gore. This prediction, made on August 29, 2000, was the closest to the actual election result of any fore-casts presented at the 2000 APSA meeting, missing Gore's 50.3 percent vote share by 2.5 percent ("Forecasts" 2000).

House Elections and the Economy

In 1996, Harvard political economist Alberto Alesina, and political scien-tists John Londregan and Howard Rosenthal—of UCLA and Princeton, respectively—offered a model to forecast presidential elections based on the outcome of Congressional elections and performance of the economy during the election year (1996). This model, in some respects similar to that of Lewis-Beck and Rice (1992) noted previously, is derived from the authors' more comprehensive theory of the electorate's preference for divided government (1993), mentioned in Chapter 6. The essence of the concept is that the electorate—particularly the voter in the moderate cen-ter—tends to balance control of Congress and of the presidency. That is, when the candidate of a party for president wins the White House, two years later the electorate reduces seats of that party in the House (the mid-term election effect). When one party controls Congress, the electorate will tend to choose a president from the other party. The effect of the electorate's behavior, therefore, is to moderate the influence of any one party on gov-ernment policy.

In the presidential election forecasting model by Alesina and colleagues, reported in Table 9.3, the performance of the president's party in the previ-ous **mid-term Congressional election** influences the vote for president. Based on their theory, one would expect the relationship to be negative. That is, if the president's party performs well in mid-term elections, this would adversely affect the fortunes of that party in the next presidential election. On the other hand, a weak result at mid-term would be a favorable sign for the party in the next election for president.

Of the model's two mid-term election indicators, one is negative as antic-ipated, but the other is positive. The share of House *seats* held by members of the president's party is negatively linked to the vote for that party's candidate for president. The unexpected positive relationship is between the *vote* share received by candidates of the president's party in all House districts and the vote garnered by that party in the next presidential election. Specifically, the vote for the incumbent party candidate for president tends to increase fol-lowing an increase in the vote for that party in the preceding mid-term House elections. Similarly, a decrease in the party's presidential vote follows a decrease in its House vote.

This positive link between votes for a party for the House and for pres-ident appears contrary to the theory of Alesina et al. The explanation could in part be statistical. The two Congressional variables are theoretically quite similar, for composition of the House at the time of a presidential election is a direct consequence of the previous mid-term election. Thus these two variables, House seats and House votes, may be highly correlated, measur-ing much the same phenomena. If so, this could help explain the unexpected difference in signs for the two variables' coefficients.

The third and final variable in this equation is the election year's annual **economic growth rate** (defined by the authors in a prior article as growth in gross national product [1993]). The growth rate indicator covers the entire election year and thus must itself be forecast to produce an election forecast.

The equation, derived from 1916–1992 data, explains 61 percent of variation in the presidential vote. Thus by comparison, this model is not as strong as most others, although the series of elections included is longer than most. The prediction by Alesina et al. for the 1996 election, which used a consensus forecast for that year's economic growth, was a 50-50 split between Clinton and Dole (1996, 123). The authors reported no standard error for the regression. Therefore, the forecast confidence interval was unknown, though undoubtedly large.

Prior Voting Patterns and the Economy

In his paper presented at the 1996 APSA meeting, Helmut Norpoth of SUNY, Stony Brook, relied primarily on combinations of economic variables and voting patterns in prior presidential elections. Norpoth computed multivariate equations for three time periods: 1872–1992, 1912–1992, and 1948–1992. The model that he chose to make the final forecast for the 1996 election was derived from data in the middle period, 1912–1992. This equation, reported in Table 9.3, includes five variables, positively or negatively related to the vote for the incumbent party candidate:

- **GNP growth** for the election year (positive)
- **Inflation rate** for the election year (negative)
- A dummy variable indicating whether the candidate of the incumbent president's party won his party's **first presidential primary election** of the election season (positive)
- Vote share received by the incumbent president's party in the **presidential election *four* years earlier** (positive)
- Vote share received by the incumbent president's party in the **presidential election *eight* years earlier** (negative)

The signs for the variables, other than the two for prior elections, are as expected. The relationship of the prior election variables to the incumbent vote is perhaps less clear. The most likely explanation proposed by Norpoth is a variant of the two-term penalty originally suggested by Abramowitz (1988), described previously. The vote for the incumbent party candidate in the election four years earlier is positively linked to that party's vote in the current election because the electorate tends to give the president (or his party) two terms. As Norpoth states, "In judging a new administration after one term, the electorate appears more inclined to give the new regime the benefit of the doubt than seize on its failures" (1996, 449). However, after two terms, "as infatuation gives way to fatigue in the electorate, incumbency turns from boon to bane for the party in the White House" (1996, 450). This model, based on data from 21 elections, had an adjusted R^2 of .77, thus accounting for 77 percent of the variation in results of those previous elections.

In generating forecasts from this model for 1996, values for three of the five causal variables were available far before the election. The two economic variables, however, cover the entire election year and thus must be estimated. For this purpose, Norpoth chose to rely on actual reported economic data available at the time of his forecast. Values for the economic indicators thus covered the 12 months from July of the year prior to the election through June of the election year. Following this approach, Norpoth predicted in early August that Clinton would receive 57.1 percent of the 1996 two-party vote, which was 2.4 percent higher than Clinton's actual vote share (1996, 534).

For the 2000 election, Norpoth substantially modified his 1996 forecasting model (Norpoth 2000b). He dropped the two economic indicators previously described and created a new measure of support in presidential primary elections, which increased the performance requirements for sitting presidents. In essence, when an incumbent president is running for reelection, he must garner more than 60 percent of the New Hampshire primary vote if the primary indicator is to operate in his favor. (For elections prior to 1952, the indicator includes all presidential primaries.) When the incumbent president is not a candidate, the 60 percent threshold does not apply. Norpoth retained the two prior election variables unchanged. His prediction for 2000, made on July 26, was that Gore would receive 55.0 percent of the two-party vote, which was 4.7 percent higher than Gore's actual 50.3 percent vote share ("Forecasts" 2000).

Norpoth made alternative predictions of the 1996 and 2000 elections from models that included only vote shares in the previous two elections, variables described previously. The forecast results were close to the actual outcomes, especially in 2000 when the prediction was off only 0.5 percent (Norpoth 2000b). (For details, see Chapter 6.)

State Level Models

To this point, the models described in this chapter all use national level data for a series of election years to explain and predict national presidential election outcomes. In this section, the focus shifts to state elections for president and influences on voting within the states.

The objective of producing a forecast of the national presidential vote remains. But rather than forecasting the national outcome directly, in this approach, a single regression equation is developed, which links economic and other conditions in all of the included states with the election results in those states and does so for several elections. For each state, the analyst weights the percentage vote forecast for a party's candidate by the estimated voter turnout. The number of supporters predicted to vote for a party's candidate in each state is then added together for all states to produce a forecast of that party's national vote. Or, to obtain a prediction of the national electoral vote, one merely determines which party's candidate is forecast to win each state, assigns the appropriate number of electoral votes to each state, and adds the state totals.

Rosenstone's Model

The first analyst to apply this pooled time-series regression technique to forecasting presidential elections was Steven Rosenstone (1983), then of Yale University, now of the University of Minnesota. His model sought to predict the Democratic candidate's share of the two-party vote nationally by pre-dicting that candidate's vote share in the respective states. The model was derived from data of the 1948–1972 time period, which included seven pres-idential elections, or 343 elections within states, the latter being the cases for the statistical analysis. Rosenstone's equation included a dummy vari-able identifying each state and five categories of substantive indicators: **social issues, state of the economy, incumbency, candidates' home states or regions**, and **party's strength in Congressional elections**. Most prominent among the social issues were those related to New Deal social welfare and racial problems.

For the New Deal social welfare category, Rosenstone identified several indicators of **social welfare liberalism**: size of a state's bureaucracy, em-ployer contributions rate for unemployment insurance, education expendi-tures per pupil, payments for Aid to Families with Dependent Children (AFDC), and state expenditures for public welfare programs. With these data for the various states in the respective election years, Rosenstone determined the extent that the indicators varied together or, conversely, represented dif-ferent aspects of social welfare liberalism. For this purpose, he used the data reduction technique of factor analysis, which produced new composite indi-cators of social welfare liberalism for each state.

Rosenstone's next step was to rank the presidential candidates on a social liberalism scale for the various elections. To do this, he enlisted the assistance of prominent historians and political scientists, knowledgeable of the candi-dates' issue positions. Each state's social liberalism score for a given election was then matched with the scores of the candidates in that election on social liberalism issues. Thus, an indicator emerged that reflected the extent of each state's support for the Democratic candidate in each election on the social lib-eralism issue dimension. (As I noted, the objective of the model was to explain the vote for that party's candidate.)

Racial liberalism scores were calculated in a similar way. State scores were the ratio of income of Blacks to income of Whites within the state. The panel of experts that rated the candidates on social liberalism rated them on this dimension as well. The scores for states and the scores for candidates were matched to produce a measure of state support for candidates on this issue dimension.

Two other issue variables also were included in Rosenstone's equation, Catholicism and public support for the government's management of wars. Catholicism was measured by percent of population that is Catholic. The war issue was measured by percent of population opposing the incumbent admin-istration's handling of the war in question, indicated by polls. These variables were narrow in their application. The Catholicism issue was used only for the 1960 election in which Kennedy's Catholic religion was an issue. The war indi-cator was applied only in 1952 (a Korean War year) and 1968 (a Vietnam War year).

The equation that resulted is reported in Table 9.4. This huge regression had 74 variables, 49 of which were dummy variables identifying the respec-tive states. It accounted for 93 percent of the variation in the states' election results and correctly identified the winner in 91 percent of the cases.

As a forecasting tool, Rosenstone's model benefits from the availability of data for most variables well before the election. However, the model is limited by including state income data for the entire election year. To produce an election forecast, one must estimate income growth for each state for the year—not an easy task. In making election forecasts for 1976 and 1980, Rosenstone dealt with this issue by using actual reported income data that were available before the election, which was for the first quarter. In effect, he assumed that first quarter income growth rates would continue for the year. His after-the-fact forecast for 1976 fared well, predicting a narrow Carter victory with 50.1 percent of the two-party vote. In fact, Carter garnered 51.0 percent of the vote for an error of only .9 percent. However, Rosenstone reports that his 1980 forecast, made three weeks before the election, was off 5.2 percent. It predicted that Carter would get 49.8 percent of the two-party vote, compared with the 44.6 percent that he actually received. Rosenstone attributes this forecast error primarily to using income data for the first quarter, after which time income fell (1983, 122).

Since the model is a pooled *state* equation, state-by-state electoral vote forecasts were possible. As one might expect after observing the popular vote results, the electoral vote forecast was close for 1976 but not for 1980. Election winners were correctly predicted, however, for each election by both popular and electoral vote forecasts.

Campbell's Model

Nine years after Rosenstone's pooled time-series model appeared, James Campbell, a prominent proponent of national level election models, published an alternative state model that used the pooled time-series approach (1992). As did Rosenstone, Campbell sought to predict the share of the two-party vote received by the Democratic candidate. Although he began with Rosenstone's work as a point of departure, he wanted to develop a less complex model than the 70-plus variable Rosenstone equation. Also, to enhance the model's usefulness in forecasting, Campbell sought variables for which all necessary data would be available prior to the November elections. The time period covered in Campbell's model was 1948 through 1988. Data included 531 cases—11 elections for 50 states, less some omissions for Alaska and Hawaii prior to statehood and southern states in 1948.

Campbell chose 16 variables, which are included in the equation in Table 9.5. As evident from the equation's beta values—in which higher values indicate greater impact on the election result—the **September trial heat polls** are the most important variable in the equation, followed by **GNP growth rate** (adjusted for incumbency) and **prior state voting patterns**. This equation accounted for 85 percent of the variation in the states' election results, and its estimates differed from the actual results by an average of only 3.02 percent.

In 1992, Campbell forecast the November election using data available at the end of July (Campbell and Mann 1992). Necessary data were available except for the early September trial heat results, which he estimated would favor Clinton by 55 percent. (When the results became available, this estimate was 2.5 percent too low.) On this basis, Campbell correctly predicted a victory

Table 9.4 ROSENSTONE'S POOLED STATE MODEL, 1948–1972

Variable	Coefficient (Slope)	Standard Error
New Deal social welfare issues		
North '48, '60, '64, '72	.099	.037
North '68	.181	.061
South '60, '64, '68, '72	.209	.085
Racial issues		
North '48, '64, '72	.081	.047
North '68	.171	.068
South '52, '68, '72	.974	.154
South '56, '60	.694	.211
South '64	1.566	.126
South '48, '68 (third party)	.440	.093
Change in real disposable income per capita *times* party	.701	.143
Change in real disposable income per capita (squared)	−2.422	1.062
Incumbent president	.041	.032
Incumbent president *times* vote for opposition party for House, previous mid-term election	.096	.034
Incumbent vice president	.039	.018
Home state presidential candidate	.039	.013
Home state vice presidential candidate	.025	.014
Home state third-party presidential candidate	−.091	.037
Southern presidential candidate	.027	.019
Catholic population (1960 only)	.109	.056
Mismanagement of war (public opinion, 1952, 1968)	−.156	.079
Vote for Democrats for House, previous mid-term election	.507	.176
Vote for Democrats for House, previous mid-term election (squared)	−.209	.143
Uncontested congressional seats, previous mid-term election	−.036	.029
Incumbent congressional seats, previous mid-term election	.031	.011
Incumbent congressional seats, previous mid-term election, *times* time	−.009	.002
State intercepts		
Nebraska	−.096	.019
Idaho	−.088	.018
Kansas	−.088	.019
Vermont	−.088	.020
Oklahoma	−.068	.019
Utah	−.064	.018
Arizona	−.055	.019
Wyoming	−.055	.019
New Hampshire	−.051	.019
Colorado	−.050	.019

(continued)

Table 9.4 (CONTINUED)

Variable	Coefficient (Slope)	Standard Error
Nevada	−.050	.019
Indiana	−.050	.019
Maine	−.044	.019
Illinois	−.041	.019
Iowa	−.038	.019
New Mexico	−.038	.019
New Jersey	−.036	.019
Montana	−.033	.019
North Dakota	−.033	.019
Wisconsin	−.032	.019
South Dakota	−.030	.020
Washington	−.024	.018
Ohio	−.024	.018
Alaska	−.023	.025
Oregon	−.023	.019
Connecticut	−.021	.019
Maryland	−.020	.018
Kentucky	−.014	.019
New York	−.014	.019
Pennsylvania	−.011	.018
Michigan	−.010	.018
Missouri	−.001	.019
Minnesota	.006	.019
Delaware	.007	.018
Hawaii	.008	.025
West Virginia	.022	.019
Rhode Island	.034	.020
Massachusetts	.042	.020
Virginia	.063	.024
Tennessee	.071	.023
Florida	.076	.026
Texas	.104	.027
Louisiana	.126	.033
North Carolina	.133	.024
Mississippi	.135	.034
Arkansas	.149	.029
Alabama	.154	.031
South Carolina	.158	.032
Georgia	.177	.030
Constant	.311	.062

Rho (1956, 1972)   .22
R^2 .93
Standard error   .045
Number of cases   343

Dependent variable: Democratic candidate's share of two-party vote

Source: Steven J. Rosenstone, *Forecasting Presidential Elections* (New Haven: Yale University Press, 1983), pp. 74–75 [slightly modified]. Copyright 1983 by Yale University Press. Reprinted by permission.

Table 9.5 Campbell's Pooled State Model, 1948–1988

Independent Variable	Coefficient	Standard Error	Beta
Constant (slope)	26.239	1.212	—
National variables:			
Democratic trial heat percentage	.449	.026	.409
2nd quarter GNP growth *times* incumbent party	2.318	.160	.322
Elected incumbent seeking reelection	1.550	.318	.118
State variables:			
State vote deviation from national vote in presidential election 4 years earlier (adjusted)	.321	.033	.263
State vote deviation from national vote in presidential election 8 years earlier (adjusted)	.263	.028	.244
Presidential home state advantage	6.671	.995	.119
Vice presidential home state advantage	2.485	.942	.046
State legislature party division 2 years earlier	.047	.010	.115
Standardized 1st qtr. state economic growth *times* incumbent party	.632	.173	.064
State liberalism index (Americans for Democratic Action and American Conservative Union)	.035	.005	.126
Regional variables:			
Presidential home region (southern) advantage	7.308	.994	.150
Southern state (1964)	−8.646	1.715	−.115
Deep South state (1964)	−17.030	2.748	−.131
New England state (1960 and 1964)	7.739	1.193	.118
Rocky Mountain West state (1976 and 1980)	−6.938	.977	−.132
North Central state (1972)	5.412	1.350	.072

Number of cases: 531
R^2 .848 (.843 adjusted)
Standard error of estimate 3.857
Mean absolute error 3.020

Dependent variable: Democratic candidate's share of two-party vote within each state.

Note: Partisan divisions (e.g., presidential vote %) involve only the two major parties. Except for regional trends, positive values on each variable favor Democratic presidential candidates. Regional trends are dummy variables ("1" for states in the region for the specified year[s] and "0" otherwise). The adjustment to the prior presidential vote deviations include the temporary prior state and regional (southern) presidential and vice presidential advantages.

Source: James E. Campbell, "Forecasting the Presidential Vote in the States," *American Journal of Political Science* vol. 36, no. 2, May 1992, p. 399 [modified]. Copyright 1992. Reprinted by permission of the University of Wisconsin Press.

for Democrat Clinton over Republican Bush, giving Clinton a close win in the two-party popular vote with 50.3 percent, but a decisive 101 vote margin in the electoral college. The popular vote forecast for Clinton was 3.2 percent too low, accounted for in part by the low estimate of Clinton's standing in the early September trial heat. Campbell's forecast of the electoral college result was **off only one electoral vote**, 371 predicted versus 370 in fact.

Scenarios for the 2000 Election Using a Multivariate Model: Conditional Forecasts by Abramowitz

For most of the models described in this chapter, it is assumed that current data for the causal variables are available to the forecaster and are used to generate the election forecasts. The models by Fair are an exception. They are designed to use projections for some indicators because the actual reported figures are not released until close to the election. In Fair's case, his well-regarded econometric model of the U.S. economy is a ready source of forecasts of the economic variables used in his election forecast model. But suppose that data for the variables, or reliable predictions for them, are not available. Or suppose that the forecaster wishes to determine the likely impact on the election of alternative values for the causal indicators. For these purposes one could turn to the scenario approach. Using that technique, the analyst merely inserts various hypothetical values for the indicators into the forecasting equation and calculates the resulting effects on the election outcome. The results from this approach are not true *ex ante* forecasts representing the analyst's one best prediction for an upcoming election. Rather, they are "conditional" forecasts of various alternative futures, conditioned on the assumption that the selected values for the causal variables occur—which may or may not happen.

In previous chapters, I showed how conditional forecasts, or scenarios, could be used when election outcomes are linked to one variable that influences the result. In this section, I illustrate how a model having two or more causal variables can project scenarios of possible election results.

In choosing a model for this purpose, from among those presented in this chapter, I have been guided by these selection criteria: high explanatory power, evident from the R^2 value; reliable variables that accurately reflect and consistently measure what they purport to; a good forecasting track record; and indicators that are readily available, understandable, and easy to calculate.

On the basis of these criteria, the model selected is that developed by Alan Abramowitz. As noted earlier in this chapter, in the fall of 2000, Abramowitz presented a specific forecast of the 2000 election outcome, 53.2 percent for Gore (two-party vote share). In 1998, however, using virtually the same equation, Abramowitz prepared conditional forecast scenarios for the 2000 election to be included in *Before the Vote* (Abramowitz 2000). It is these scenarios that I describe in this section.

The forecasts produced by Abramowitz are of the share of the two-party vote received by the candidate of the incumbent president's party. In the 2000 election, since the incumbent was a Democrat, conditional forecasts from the model were the percent of the two-party vote that might have been received by the Democratic candidate, Al Gore.

As we saw in the earlier description in this chapter, the Abramowitz model includes three causal variables: presidential approval ratings in early July of the election year, GDP growth rate for the first half of the year, and an indicator denoting whether the president's party has occupied the White House for two terms. The GDP data are annualized, reflecting what the annual growth rate would be if the rate for the first half continued the entire year. The two-term indicator is used by Abramowitz to capture voter sentiment that it is—in his words—"time for a change" after one party has occupied the White House for eight years. For the 2000 election, this two-term penalty existed since incumbent President Clinton was finishing his second term. This then was a factor militating against the candidate of his party, Vice President Gore.

Using these indicators, Abramowitz computed the following equation (Abramowitz 2000, 54). It is derived from data for the 1948–1996 election years and thus is appropriate for calculating forecast scenarios for the 2000 election.

$$
\begin{aligned}
\text{incumbent \textbf{(Gore)}} \\
\text{share of two-party} \; &= \; 40.634 \; + \; (.220 \times \text{pres. app. rating}_{\text{early July}}) \\
\textbf{vote} \text{ in \textbf{2000}} \quad & \qquad + \; (.900 \times \text{ann. GDP growth}_{\text{1st half}}) \\
& \qquad - \; (3.886 \times \text{two-term penalty})
\end{aligned}
$$

EQUATION **9.1**

R^2 .909 (adjusted)
t-values for indicators
    4.49, 4.84, −3.30 (respectively)
    (significance for each .01)

standard error for indicators
    .049, .186, 1.177 (respectively)
standard error for equation 1.800
number of elections 13 (1948–1996)

In 1998, Abramowitz produced conditional forecasts for the 2000 election by inserting various combinations of values for the presidential approval rating and for GDP growth into this equation. In Table 9.6 the presidential approval scores range from 40 to 65 percent, at intervals of 5 percent. For GDP growth rate in the first half, the values vary from −1 to +5 percent (annualized) at 1 percent intervals. The value for the two-term penalty variable is the same in each scenario. A "one" was entered into the equation for this negative indicator, since, as noted, the penalty was in effect in 2000.

Suppose, for example, that Clinton's expected July approval rating was 55 percent, and that the predicted annualized GDP growth rate in the first half of 2000 was 2 percent. What share of the two-party vote would Gore then be expected to receive? The result is calculated as follows by inserting these numbers into equation 9.1 along with a "one" for the two-term penalty:

Table 9.6 Abramowitz Model: Conditional Forecast Scenarios for 2000 Election, Percent of Two-Party Vote for Democratic Candidate

Annualized GDP Growth 1st Half 2000 (%)	Clinton Approval Rating Early July 2000 (%)					
	40	45	50	55	60	65
−1	44.6	45.7	46.8	47.9	49.0	50.1
0	45.5	46.6	47.7	48.8	49.9	51.0
1	46.4	47.5	48.6	49.7	50.8	51.9
2	47.3	48.4	49.5	50.6	51.7	52.8
3	48.2	49.3	50.4	51.5	52.6	53.7
4	49.1	50.2	51.3	52.4	53.5	54.6
5	50.0	51.1	52.2	53.3	54.4	55.5

Note: The two-term penalty variable was included in the calculations and is negative for the Democratic candidate since that party has occupied the White House for two terms.

Source: Alan I. Abramowitz, "Bill and Al's Excellent Adventure: Forecasting the 1996 Presidential Election," in *Before the Vote: Forecasting American National Elections*, eds. James E. Campbell and James C. Garand (Thousand Oaks, CA: Sage Publications, 2000), p. 56. Copyright 2000 by Sage Publications, Inc. Reprinted by permission of Sage Publications, Inc.

$$\text{incumbent (Gore) share of two-party vote in 2000} = 40.634 + (.220 \times 55 \ [\text{pres. app. rating}_{\text{early July}}])$$
$$+ (.900 \times 2 \ [\text{ann. GDP growth}_{\text{1st half}}])$$
$$- (.3.886 \times 1 \ [\text{two-term penalty}])$$
$$= 40.634 + 12.100 + 1.800 - 3.886$$
$$= 50.6\%$$

We find this estimate of Gore's vote share, 50.6 percent, in Table 9.6 by observing the point at which a presidential approval rating of 55 percent intersects with the 2 percent GDP growth rate. This pattern is followed throughout the table. Taking another example, suppose that the economy was expected to be more robust, growing at an annual rate of 4 percent. Assuming the same 55 percent presidential approval rating, the table shows that Gore's share of the two-party vote would likely rise to 52.4 percent.

In studying Table 9.6 we see that, although alternative values for the causal indicators vary across rather wide ranges of scores, the effect on the vote is modest. Small changes in the indicators have even smaller effects on the election. Specifically, in equation 9.1 the slope for the president's approval rating is .220. This means that if Clinton's job rating increases one percentage point, the resultant increase in the vote for Gore is only 0.220 percent. This effect is, of course, evident in the table. Again notice that Abramowitz has listed the hypothetical approval ratings in five-point increments. If 0.220 is multiplied by 5, that result (1.1 percent) is the difference in Gore's vote for a 5 percent change in Clinton's approval rating, evident as we move horizontally across the table. Similarly, in equation 9.1, we see that a 1 percent increase in GDP results in 0.9 percent increase in the vote received by Gore (because the slope for GDP is 0.9). Thus in Table 9.6, the difference in the Gore vote is 0.9

percent for each 1 percent change on the vertical scale, as we look up and down in the table.

In the worse case scenario (top-left corner of the table), Gore would be expected to garner no less than 44.6 percent of the two-party vote. In the best case scenario (bottom-right corner), Gore would get no more than 55.5 percent of the vote. This is a range of 10.9 percent percent in election results across the scenarios. The table is structured so that at its center, where values at the mid-point of the indicators' ranges appear, the vote is rather equally divided.

As I conclude this description of conditional forecast scenarios, it is important to recall that these predictions are hypothetical. They are based on assumed values for the causal variables, not factual data. Tables, like that by Abramowitz, present an array of scenarios that can be useful in making long-range projections when actual data are not yet available. They also are helpful in assessing the impact on the election of changes in the variables.

Conclusion

In this chapter, I have described a wide range of multivariate models that have been developed to forecast presidential elections. As might be expected, they include a variety of indicators, which a glance at the tables reveals. Although the indicators that have appeared in one model or another are many and varied, the rationale for including most of them stems from a common assumption: Presidential elections are public referenda on whether to retain the incumbent party in the White House. If the public is satisfied with "the way things are going," they tend to keep the incumbent president's party in office; if not, they are inclined to make a change. That is the key assumption underlying the forecasting models.

To the forecasters who crafted these models, the party of the president has little significance for the outcome. Characteristics of the candidates are also of little importance, as are campaigns. In these models, it does not matter whether the president is a Democrat or Republican. Nor does it matter whether a party's nominee runs an effective fall campaign. What does matter is whether people are satisfied with the present state of affairs. If so, they are likely to keep the president, or his successor as party nominee, on the job.

In this chapter, we have seen this incumbency theme in the forecasters' choice of variables. The two-term penalty indicator explicitly assumes that the public penalizes the incumbent president's party after two terms in office by not returning it for a third term. That is, after a point incumbency becomes detrimental. Indicators that measure the health of the economy can predict election results because the public tends to give credit or blame to the incumbent president, and then reward or punish him—or other candidate of his party—at the polls. The electoral impact of the president's job approval ratings is similar. If the public approves of the president's performance, he or his successor candidate is likely to benefit in the next election.

This emphasis on incumbency is most evident in the national level models. More variety of indicators is possible at the state level, as the two pooled time-series state models demonstrate.

Are the assumptions underlying these models—especially the national ones—too limited, too narrow? Omitting such important electoral influences as parties and campaigns seems difficult to justify. On the other hand, most of the recent models have performed well in predicting election outcomes–that is, until the 2000 election, which I now consider.

Conclusion:
A Forecasting Perspective
of the 2000 Election

After the 1996 presidential election, forecasters were riding high. Nearly all had predicted the Clinton victory. Most had done so with a high degree of accuracy, and the entire forecasting enterprise seemed to gain in stature and credibility. Not surprisingly, as the 2000 election approached, reporters were interested in the forecasters' election predictions, even encouraging them to release early estimates (Kaiser 2000b). There was considerable interest in the academic community as well, which was evident in the well-attended forecasters' session at the American Political Science Association (APSA) meeting at the end of August.

Then came election night 2000, and the results were a very close win for Democrat Al Gore in the popular vote. But for Gore, it was a hollow victory. For the first time in more than a century, the winner of the popular vote failed to win the Electoral College and thus did not become president. With the Supreme Court effectively deciding the election in a dispute over marred ballots in Florida, this was one of the strangest elections ever, as Republican George W. Bush became the new president.

How accurate were forecasts in this difficult electoral setting? As seen in previous chapters, simple win-loss line plots did rather well, with most—not all—accurately predicting Gore as the winner of the popular vote. Simple regressions using one independent variable mostly predicted the winner correctly, too, although the vote percentages for Gore tended to be too high, and forecast margins of error were large. Historian Allan Lichtman likewise predicted a Gore popular vote victory, continuing his string of correct calls in presidential elections. Although the Lichtman scheme does not produce percentage estimates, his prediction for Gore was decided by the closest margin possible. Economist Ray Fair's multivariate regression model generated an extraordinarily accurate forecast in 2000, predicting Gore as the popular vote winner and missing his share of the vote by only 0.5 percent.

Political science forecasters, who presented predictions from their multivariate models at the APSA meeting shortly before Labor Day, were all correct in anticipating Gore's win in the popular vote. However, most of their estimates were far too optimistic for Gore, ranging from 52.8 percent to 60.3 percent of the two-party vote, when in fact Gore garnered only 50.3 percent.

Impediments to Predicting the 2000 Election

A few months after the election, forecasters in political science published remarkably candid self-evaluations of their work. These articles appeared in the March 2001 issue of *PS: Political Science and Politics* and in the May 2001 issue of *American Politics Research*. (They are listed in the Bibliography as entries for Abramowitz, Campbell, Holbrook, Lewis-Beck and Tien, Locker-bie, Norpoth, Wlezien, and Wlezien and Erikson.)

As these scholars reviewed the election, critiquing their work, they tentatively identified several possible reasons for the models' large forecast errors favoring Gore. Among the reasons mentioned were the following:

- Gore's campaign strategy and performance
- Reluctance of voters to give Gore full credit for the strong economy that had existed during most of Clinton's presidency
- The economic slowdown after mid-year
- President Clinton's personal problems
- The tendency of voters to change parties in the White House after two terms
- The candidacy of Ralph Nader, who may have taken voters away from Gore

In the sections that follow, I describe these factors that appear to have impeded the forecasting effort in 2000. I have chosen items mentioned by more than one forecaster and present them in greater detail and perhaps with more conviction than appeared in the articles. Most of the possible reasons for the forecast errors were proposed quite tentatively by analysts who seemed to be searching for causes rather than stating definitive explanations.

Gore's Campaign

It is commonly believed that Al Gore's campaign strategy and performance were ineffective in presenting his candidacy. This contention should be viewed from the perspective of research on fall presidential campaigns discussed in Chapter 7. There we saw that campaigns have an important role in elections, but usually not a large direct impact on election results. Campaigns are important primarily in stimulating voters' interest in the candidates and, through their intense competition, sharply focusing voters' attention on underlying factors that, in turn, influence the voting decision. Typically, campaigns function effectively in this respect as an indirect influence on elections, having little independent effect on the results. Consequently, it usually has not been necessary for the forecaster to account for campaign performance in order to accurately predict election outcomes; forecasts can be based on the underlying influences that predate the campaign.

However, the Gore campaign in 2000 may have been less effective than usual in performing the expected function of campaigns. In particular, it appears that Gore failed to stimulate voter awareness of conditions favorable to him—especially the strong economy—and was unable to adequately mobilize voters in support of the Gore cause. Although he was the candidate of the incumbent president's party, Gore seemed reluctant to be linked even to the positive results of the president's administration; apparently, he wanted to distance himself from negatives associated with Clinton. As a result, forecasting models based on the assumption of effective campaigns may have produced inaccurate predictions because of the Gore campaign's lackluster performance.

None of the forecasting models was able to account for atypical campaign behavior, for none included a campaign variable. However, the model of James Campbell does include early September trial heat polls of the candidates' standing with the public, which is in effect a precampaign variable. Following the 2000 election, Campbell (2001a, 291) calculated alternative versions of his model by replacing the early September trial heat indicator with trial heats made during the fall campaign—in late September, October, and early November. He found that the models that included trial heat polls during the campaign improved his predictions significantly by reducing Gore's estimated share of the vote. This result may have reflected Gore's campaign performance in the fall, although other factors, such as the downturn in the economy during this period, could have been influential too.

Performance of the Economy

According to assumptions stated in Chapter 8, the strong economy in years preceding the 2000 election should have led to a solid electoral victory for the incumbent party candidate, Al Gore. In that chapter, I noted evidence that voters are influenced by economic conditions in the past. When the economy has performed well, benefiting voters, they tend to give the president credit. As a consequence, they will likely vote to keep the president's party in the White House, hoping that the good times continue. If the economy has performed poorly, the effect is comparably negative.

In 2000, the economy continued its robust performance trend through the second quarter—the end of June. After that time, however, the election year economy dropped significantly, from a 5.6 percent growth rate in the second quarter to a 2.2 percent growth rate in the third quarter.

Most forecasting models used economic data ending with the second quarter and predicted an overly optimistic result for Gore. Economic explanations of the models' high estimates for Gore have taken two forms: First, voters may not have given Gore full credit for the strong economic growth that existed during most of the Clinton administration. Second, voters may have been influenced by the economic downturn that began in the third quarter, diluting the impact of the favorable economic conditions existing through the second quarter.

Let us look first at the position that voters failed to give Gore credit for the strong economy of the Clinton years. On one hand, Gore may have fostered this result during the campaign by his reluctance to claim credit for the positive outcomes of the Clinton presidency, as I mentioned in the previous section. On the other hand, perhaps voters give full credit for a strong economy only to an incumbent president, which would have hurt nonincumbent Gore. After the election, Campbell (2001a, 293) tested the latter concept by manipulating the impact of the second quarter economic growth variable in his model. He found that when Gore was given *full* credit for economic conditions, Gore's predicted two-party vote was 52.8 percent (2.5% too high). When Gore was given only *half* credit for the economy, the forecast improved, with a lower predicted vote for Gore. Giving Gore *no* credit for the economy produced the best forecast of all, an even lower vote share, 50.3 percent (a perfect prediction). It appears, therefore, that voters were unwilling to give Gore credit for the good economic times of the Clinton years, which likely reduced his vote in the election.

As for the second point, voters may have been influenced by the economic slowdown that began in the third quarter. If so, this might account for inaccurate predictions produced by forecasting models that could account for economic conditions only through the robust second quarter. Economist Ray Fair's highly accurate forecasts in 2000 provide evidence supporting the impact of third-quarter economic conditions. Fair's model uses economic data for the first three quarters of the election year, and it turned in the best forecasting performance of any model in 2000. Fair (2000) predicted a 50.8 percent vote for Gore, only 0.5 percent in error. (Of course, including the third quarter for his economic variables meant that Fair had to predict economic conditions in the third quarter, which his model of the U.S. economy did accurately.)

The Public's Evaluation of President Clinton

President Clinton's job approval ratings were strong before the 2000 election, but candidate Gore did not appear to reap the expected benefit. Forecasting models that included job approval ratings predicted a higher vote for Gore than he received. In fact, Gore's very narrow popular vote win seemed to cast doubt on the strength of assumptions, noted in Chapter 3, that voters who approve of a president's past job performance are likely to reward him by keeping his party in the White House.

Why did Gore apparently not benefit fully from Clinton's high job ratings? Perhaps it is because Gore was not the incumbent. After all, the approval rating is of the president's personal job performance, not of his party's performance. Thus, approval of the president's job may not carry over as well to someone else hoping to succeed him—an argument similar to that made previously with regard to the benefit of a good economy for a nonincumbent candidate.

In addition, the benefit to Gore of Clinton's strong job ratings may have been diluted by the president's personal problems—"the Clinton factor." Perhaps voters evaluate a president as a "whole person," both job performance and personal traits. Normally, a president's personal behavior is acceptable to the public and thus of little importance to voters in a presidential election. This was true in the post–World War II period on which most of the forecasting models were constructed. However, President Clinton's personal behavior, unlike that of his post–World War II predecessors, generally was viewed as not acceptable. What had been a latent influence on voters became an active influence.

Evidence from the 2000 election exit polls reveals that Gore likely did not benefit as much from the president's strong approval ratings as he would have if "the Clinton factor" had not been an issue. In his post-election analysis, Abramowitz notes that in exit polls taken on election day,

> . . . there was an extraordinary split in voters' opinions about President Clinton. On one hand, 57% of the voters approved of President Clinton's job performance, and only 41% disapproved. On the other hand, only 36% of the same voters had a favorable opinion of Bill Clinton as a person, whereas 60% had an unfavorable opinion (Abramowitz 2001, 279–280).

Norpoth (2001b, 47) points to more detailed exit poll results, which showed the adverse impact on Gore of voters' negative views of Clinton personally. These polls reported that 85 percent of the voters who approved of Clinton's job performance and *liked* him as a person voted for Gore. Of those who also approved of Clinton's job performance but *disliked* him as a person, only 63 percent voted for Gore. It appears, therefore, that the Clinton factor did have a negative effect on the vote for Gore. Forecasting models did not account for this, which may have contributed to their high estimates of the Gore vote.

Time for Change after Two Terms

The 2000 election underscores the tendency of voters to change parties in the White House after two terms. Since the Democrats had been in office two terms, this "time for change" phenomenon, as Abramowitz calls it, worked against Gore. As noted in Chapter 9, the two-term penalty reduces the vote of the incumbent party candidate by 4 to 5 percent, which contributed favorably to Abramowitz's 53.2 percent forecast for Gore, a relatively small 2.9 percent prediction error (Abramowitz 2001). Without the two-term adjustment, the Abramowitz forecast of Gore's vote might have been 4 or 5 percent higher, slightly above the 5.7 percent average error of the political science forecasts. In turn, some of these models' large prediction errors favoring Gore might have been reduced by accounting for the Democrats' preceding two terms in the presidency.

For the candidates, 4 or 5 percent can be of great importance in close elections like that of 2000. Suppose that Gore's race for the presidency had not followed an eight-year tenure of his party in the White House. Adding another 4 percent to his 50.3 percent share of the two-party vote would have given Gore 54.3 percent, which would have been considered a strong showing and in line with expectations based on performance of the economy to mid-year and Clinton's job approval ratings. Thus, it may be that Gore's close electoral margin was due to this simple cyclical pattern over which he had no control.

Minor Candidates—the Nader Factor

Did Ralph Nader, candidate of the Green Party, take voters away from Al Gore? Nader received less than 3 percent of the vote. However, according to exit polls, had he not been on the ballot 50 percent of Nader's voters would have voted for Gore compared with only 20 percent for Bush; 30 percent would not have voted. Building on these exit poll results, Abramowitz (2001, 281) estimates that without Nader as a candidate Gore would have gained another 1 percent of the national vote, likely carrying Florida and New Hampshire—and the Electoral College.

If in fact Nader did draw votes away from Gore, the forecasting models were unable to account for that, for they are based only on votes for candidates of the two major parties. As a result, the vote for Gore would have been overestimated.

Election forecasters have little choice but to avoid counting votes of minor party candidates or independents. Forecasting models are based on a statistical comparison of elections in the past in which minor candidates have appeared in one election, often to disappear an election or two later. As minor candidates change, so do their supporters within the electorate. As a result, their votes cannot be consistently or meaningfully tallied over time, as can votes for the Democratic and Republican candidates.

Most forecasters totally disregard votes for minor candidates in their models. In effect, they assume that if minor candidates were not on the ballot, the votes they receive would be divided between the two major party candidates in the same proportion as the vote garnered by each of the major candidates. A less common approach is to assign votes of minor candidates equally to the two major candidates. Usually these procedures have created little difficulty for forecasters, because, as we know from exit polls, supporters of minor candidates tend to split more or less equally between the major party candidates. In this respect, the Nader candidacy was unusual because it drew disproportionately from the Democrat without an offsetting candidate of comparable strength drawing from the Republican.

Alternative Approaches and Objectives

Surely one lesson from the 2000 experience is that the election forecasting enterprise would benefit from using a greater variety of prediction techniques. In 2000, nearly all of the election forecasts were produced by national-level regression models. When these models produce unrealistic results, as some did in 2000, few predictions from alternative approaches are available for comparison. However, other techniques exist that can be easily applied to contemporary efforts to predict presidential elections.

First, the use of *state-level pooled time-series models* could be revived. These models are complex and cumbersome, but they have been used with some success in the past and have considerable potential in the current setting. By providing predictions of state elections, they remind us that a presidential election is in fact 51 individual contests for each state's electoral votes (including

Washington, D.C.). Moreover, pooled state models have methodological advantages in that they do not rely on a small number of cases, which many national models do.

Second, rather than being concerned exclusively with predicting the percentage of the vote—that is, point forecasts—attention also could be given to estimating the *probability (odds) of a party's candidate winning* the election. Logistic regression (logit) is an appropriate technique for this purpose. Although I find no precedent for its use in forecasting elections, Haynes and Stone (1994, 124–125) considered a logistic approach before choosing ordinary regression for their model.

Third, one might choose to predict the election winner with less precision by using simple *line plots,* such as I presented in some preceding chapters. Recall that these are historical graphs of individual indicators' values at the time of past elections in which thresholds for a party's candidate winning or losing are identified. Line plots usually have predicted election winners correctly, and their use requires no knowledge of statistics.

Fourth, techniques based on *expert judgment* could usefully contribute to the forecasting effort. On one hand, ratings by knowledgeable experts of phenomena otherwise difficult to quantify could be used as variables in regression models, as Rosenstone (1983) has done. As an example, ratings could be made of the effectiveness of campaigns conducted by presidential candidates, historically and for the election being predicted. On the other hand, expert forecasts of election outcomes could provide credible alternatives to predictions from quantitative models. In fact, predictions of vote shares derived from approaches such as Delphi and pooled state models might be combined with national-level regression forecasts. Improved predictions could result, for when forecasts produced by different techniques are combined—even by simple averaging—typically the result is more accurate than the predictions produced by any single technique (Makridakis et al 1998, 537–542).

In addition to highlighting the desirability of bringing more techniques into the election forecasting enterprise, the 2000 experience underscores the importance of directing some effort to predicting the *electoral vote.* As we know, in 2000 the country faced a result in which one candidate won the close popular vote, and another candidate won the close electoral vote, thereby becoming president. All of the current national level models, however, attempt to predict only the popular vote; none is designed to predict the electoral vote (although in the past a model by Lewis-Beck and Rice [1992] did so). National level models could likely be developed for this purpose without great difficulty by building on knowledge gained in creating popular vote models. Moreover, as I have suggested, state-level pooled models can easily produce electoral vote estimates by assigning each state's electoral votes to the predicted state winner, as was done when these models were used in the past.

In retrospect, forecasters encountered extraordinary challenges in attempting to predict the 2000 election result: a razor-thin vote margin, dramatic change in performance of the economy during the election year, a backdrop of presidential scandal and impeachment, and other factors that I have recounted. In view of these obstacles impeding accurate predictions, it is not as surprising that some forecasts were wrong as it is that any were right. Even though election forecasters may not face such a difficult task again soon, it does seem prudent to diversify among forecasting techniques to reduce the risk of shared prediction errors resulting from similar applications of one approach. On balance, the forecasting legacy of the 2000 election is likely to be positive, as models are refined in the light of this experience and as alternative prediction techniques come into greater use.

Bibliography

Abdollahian, Mark Andrew and Jacek Kugler. 1997. "Unraveling the Ties That Divide: Russian Political Succession." *International Interactions* 23: 267–281.

Abramowitz, Alan I. 1988. "An Improved Model for Predicting Presidential Election Outcomes." *PS: Political Science and Politics* 21: 843–847.

———. 1994. "Is It Time for Them to Go? Forecasting the 1992 Presidential Election." *Political Methodologist* 5 (2): 2–3. (Available at http://web.polmeth.ufl.edu/tpm.html.)

———. 1996. "Bill and Al's Excellent Adventure: Forecasting the 1996 Presidential Election." *American Politics Quarterly* 24: 434–442; forecast addendum, 532.

———. 2000. "Bill and Al's Excellent Adventure: Forecasting the 1996 Presidential Election." In *Before the Vote: Forecasting American National Elections*. eds. James E. Campbell and James C. Garand. Thousand Oaks, CA: Sage Publications. (Update of Abramowitz 1996.)

———. 2001. "The Time for Change Model and the 2000 Election." *American Politics Research* 29: 279–282.

Adams, Henry. 1890. *History of the United States of America During the First Administration of James Madison*. v. 2. New York: Charles Scribner's Sons.

Adkins, Randall E. and Andrew J. Dowdle. 2001. "Is the Exhibition Season Becoming More Important to Forecasting Presidential Nominations?" *American Politics Research* 29: 283–288.

Alesina, Alberto, John Londregan, and Howard Rosenthal. 1993. "A Model of the Political Economy of the United States." *American Political Science Review* 87: 12–33.

———. 1996. "The 1992, 1994 and 1996 Elections: A Comment and a Forecast." *Public Choice* 88: 115–125.

"And Here Is Your Next President." 1996. *Economist* 23 December, 31–33.

Armstrong, J. Scott. 1985. *Long-Range Forecasting: From Crystal Ball to Computer*. 2d ed. New York: John Wiley and Sons.

Bartels, Larry M. and John Zaller. 2001. "Presidential Vote Models: A Recount." *PS: Political Science and Politics* 34: 9–20.

Bean, Louis H. 1948. *How to Predict Elections*. New York: Alfred A. Knopf.

———. 1968. *How America Votes in Presidential Elections*. Metuchen, NJ: Scarecrow Press.

———. 1969. *The Art of Forecasting*. New York: Random House.

———. 1972. *How to Predict the 1972 Election*. New York: Quadrangle Books.

Beck, Nathaniel. 1992. "Forecasting the 1992 Presidential Election: The Message Is in the Confidence Interval." *Public Perspective* September/October, 32–34.

———. 1994. "We Should Be Modest: Forecasting the 1992 Presidential Election." *Political Methodologist* 5 (2): 19–24. (Available at http://web.polmeth.ufl.edu/tpm.html.)

———. 2000. "Evaluating Forecasts and Forecasting Models of the 1996 Presidential Election." In *Before the Vote: Forecasting American National Elections*. eds. James E. Campbell and James C. Garand. Thousand Oaks, CA: Sage Publications.

Berry, Brian J. L., Euel Elliott, and Edward J. Harpham. 1996. "The Yield Curve As an Electoral Bellwether." *Technological Forecasting and Social Change* 51: 281–294.

Berg, Joyce E., Robert Forsythe, and Thomas A. Rietz. 1997a. "The Iowa Electronic Market." In *The Blackwell Encyclopedic Dictionary of Finance*. eds. Dean Paxson and Douglas Wood. Cambridge, MA: Blackwell Business.

———. 1997b. "What Makes Markets Predict Well? Evidence from the Iowa Electronic Markets." In *Understanding Strategic Interaction: Essays in Honor of Reinhard Selten*. eds. Wulf Albers et al. New York: Springer.

Broder, David. 1992. "Pundits' Brew: How It Looks." *Washington Post* 1 November, C1.

———. 2001. "Why Election Predictors Bombed." *Washington Post* 8 April, B7.

Brody, Richard and Lee Sigelman. 1983. "Presidential Popularity and Presidential Elections: An Update and Extension." *Public Opinion Quarterly* 47: 325–328.

Broh, C. Anthony. 1980. "Whether Bellwethers or Weather-Jars Indicate Election Outcomes." *Western Political Quarterly* 33: 564–570.

Buchanan, William. 1986. "Election Predictions: An Empirical Assessment." *Public Opinion Quarterly* 50: 222–227.

Budge, Ian and Dennis J. Farlie. 1983. *Explaining and Predicting Elections: Issue Effects and Party Strategies in Twenty-Three Democracies*. London: George Allen and Unwin.

Bueno de Mesquita, Bruce. 1994. "Political Forecasting: An Expected Utility Method." In *European Community Decision Making: Models, Applications, and Comparisons*. eds. Bruce Bueno de Mesquita and Frans N. Stokman. New Haven, CT: Yale University Press.

———. 1997. "A Decision Making Model: Its Structure and Form." *International Interactions* 23: 235–266.

Cable News Network. 2000a. "CNN, USA Today, Gallup Tracking Poll." (2000 campaign poll series available at http://www.cnn.com/2000/ALLPOLITICS/stories/11/05/tracking.poll/index.html.)

———. 2000b. "Exit Polls for Pennsylvania [in 2000 presidential election]." (Available at http://www.cnn.com/ELECTION/2000/epolls/PA/P000.html.)

Campbell, James E. 1992. "Forecasting the Presidential Vote in the States." *American Journal of Political Science* 36: 386–407.

———. 1993. "Weather Forecasters Should Be So Accurate: A Response to 'Forewarned Before Forecast'." *PS: Political Science and Politics* 26: 165–166.

———. 1996. "Polls and Votes: The Trial-Heat Presidential Election Forecasting Model, Certainty, and Political Campaigns." *American Politics Quarterly* 24: 408–433; forecast addendum, 532–533.

———. 1997. *The Presidential Pulse of Congressional Elections*. Lexington, KY: University of Kentucky Press.

———. 2000a. *The American Campaign: U.S. Presidential Campaigns and the National Vote*. College Station, TX: Texas A & M University Press.

———. 2000b. "Polls and Votes: The Trial-Heat Presidential Election Forecasting Model, Certainty, and Political Campaigns." In *Before the Vote: Forecasting American National*

Elections. eds. James E. Campbell and James C. Garand. Thousand Oaks, CA: Sage Publications. (Update of Campbell 1996.)

———. 2000c. "The Science of Forecasting Presidential Elections." In *Before the Vote: Forecasting American National Elections*. eds. James E. Campbell and James C. Garand. Thousand Oaks, CA: Sage Publications.

———. 2001a. "An Evaluation of the Trial-Heat and Economy Forecast of the Presidential Vote in the 2000 Election." *American Politics Research* 29: 289–296.

———. 2001b. "The Referendum That Didn't Happen: The Forecasts of the 2000 Presidential Election." *PS: Political Science and Politics* 34: 33–38.

———. 2001c. "Taking Stock of the Forecasts of the 2000 Presidential Election." *American Politics Research* 29: 275–278.

Campbell, James E. and James C. Garand. eds. 2000. *Before the Vote: Forecasting American National Elections*. Thousand Oaks, CA: Sage Publications.

Campbell, James E. and Thomas E. Mann. 1992. "Forecasting the 1992 Election: A User's Guide to the Models." *Brookings Review* 10 (4): 22–27.

———. 1996. "Forecasting the Presidential Election." *Brookings Review* 14 (4): 26–31.

Campbell, James E. and Kenneth A. Wink. 1990. "Trial-Heat Forecasts of the Presidential Vote." *American Politics Quarterly* 18: 251–269.

Carville, James. 1996. *We're Right, They're Wrong: A Handbook for Spirited Progressives*. New York: Random House.

Clymer, Adam. 1998. "50 Years Later, Pollsters Analyze Their Big Defeat." *New York Times* 18 May, A10.

Cohen, Jeffrey E. 1998. "State-Level Public Opinion Polls As Predictors of Presidential Election Results." *American Politics Quarterly* 26: 139–159.

Conference Board. 1999. "Table with New and Old Leading Indexes, January 1995 to October 1996." (Available at http://www.tcb-indicators.org/lei/revisions/rev96tbl.htm.)

———. 2000. "Full History (1959–present) of the Three Composite Indexes [of economic indicators] and Corresponding 6-Month Diffusion." (Available at http://www.tcb-indicators.org/leihistory/hindex.htm.)

Congressional Quarterly. 1994. *Congressional Quarterly's Guide to U.S. Elections*. 3d ed. Washington: Congressional Quarterly.

———. 1997. *Presidential Elections, 1789–1996*. Washington: Congressional Quarterly.

Cook, Charlie. 2000. "Listen to Political Scientists, But Be Wary." *National Journal* 3 June, 1776–1777.

Darnay, Arsen J. comp. and ed. 1996. *Economic Indicators Handbook*. 3d ed. Detroit: Gale Research.

Devine, Donald J. 1983. *Reagan Electionomics: How Reagan Ambushed the Pollsters*. Ottawa, IL: Green Hill Publishers.

———. 1990. "Political Science in Four Presidential Elections." *PS: Political Science and Politics* 23: 428–429.

Eckes, Alfred. 1992. "Forecasting Presidential Elections: A Historian's Perspective." *Vital Speeches of the Day* 1 May, 425–427.

Edwards, George C. III with Alec M. Gallup. 1990. *Presidential Approval: A Sourcebook*. Baltimore: Johns Hopkins University Press.

Emerson, Ralph Waldo. 1903. "The Conservative [9 December 1841]." In *Nature: Address and Lectures by Ralph Waldo Emerson*. Boston: Houghton Mifflin.

Erikson, Robert S. 1989a. "Economic Conditions and the Presidential Vote." *American Political Science Review* 83: 567–573.

———. 1989b. "Why the Democrats Lose Presidential Elections: Toward a Theory of Optimal Loss." *PS: Political Science and Politics* 22: 30–35.

———. 1999. "Presidential Polls As a Time Series: The Case of 1996." *Public Opinion Quarterly* 63: 163–177.

Erikson, Robert S. and Christopher Wlezien. 1996. "Of Time and Presidential Election Forecasts." *PS: Political Science and Politics* 29: 37–39.

Ezra, Marni and Candice J. Nelson. 1995. "Do Campaigns Matter?" In *Campaigns and Elections American Style*. ed. James A. Thurber and Candice J. Nelson. Boulder, CO: Westview Press.

Fackler, Tim and Tse-min Lin. 1995. "Political Corruption and Presidential Elections, 1929–1992." *Journal of Politics* 57: 971–993.

Fair, Ray C. 1978. "The Effect of Economic Events on Votes for President." *Review of Economics and Statistics* 60: 159–173.

———. 1982. "The Effect of Economic Events on Votes for President: 1980 Results." *Review of Economics and Statistics* 64: 322–325.

———. 1988. "The Effect of Economic Events on Votes for President: 1984 Update." *Political Behavior* 10: 168–179.

———. 1996a. "Econometrics and Presidential Elections." *Journal of Economic Perspectives* 10: 89–102.

———. 1996b. "The Effect of Economic Events on Votes for President: 1992 Update." *Political Behavior* 18: 119–139.

———. 1998. "The Effect of Economic Events on Votes for President: 1996 Update." 6 November. (Available at http://fairmodel.econ.yale.edu/RAYFAIR/PDF/1998AHTM.HTM.)

———. 2000. "Presidential Vote Equation." (Available at http://fairmodel.econ.yale.edu/vote/.)

Feder, Stanley A. 1995. "Factions and Policon: New Ways to Analyze Politics." In *Inside CIA's Private World: Declassified Articles from the Agency's Internal Journal, 1955–1992*. ed. H. Bradford Westerfield. New Haven: Yale University Press.

Field, Mervin D. 1983. "Political Opinion Polling in the United States of America." In *Political Opinion Polling: An International Review*. ed. Robert M. Worcester. New York: St. Martin's Press.

Finkel, Steven E., Thomas M. Guterbock, and Marian J. Borg. 1991. "Race-of-Interviewer Effects in a Preelection Poll: Virginia, 1989." *Public Opinion Quarterly* 55: 313–330.

Fiorina, Morris P. 1981. *Retrospective Voting in American National Elections*. New Haven: Yale University Press.

"Forecasts of the 2000 Presidential Election Based on the Forecasting Models in Campbell and Garand's *Before the Vote* (Sage Publications, 2000)." 2000. Table presented at the annual meeting of the American Political Science Association. Washington, D.C.

Forsythe, Robert, Forrest Nelson, and George R. Neumann. 1994. "The Iowa Political Stock Markets: September Forecasts." *Political Methodologist* 5 (2): 15–18. (Available at http://web.polmeth.ufl.edu/tpm.html.)

Forsythe, Robert, Forrest Nelson, George R. Neumann, and Jack Wright. 1992. "Anatomy of an Experimental Political Stock Market." *American Economic Review* 82: 1142–1161.

Galbraith, John Kenneth. 1990. *A Tenured Professor: A Novel*. Boston: Houghton Mifflin.

Gallup, George H. 1972. *The Gallup Poll: Public Opinion 1935–1971*. vols. 1, 2, 3. New York: Random House.

———. 1978. *The Gallup Poll: Public Opinion 1972–1977*. vols. 1, 2. Wilmington, DE: Scholarly Resources.

———. 1981. *The Gallup Poll: Public Opinion 1980*. Wilmington, DE: Scholarly Resources.

Gallup, George Jr. 1985. *The Gallup Poll: Public Opinion 1984*. Wilmington, DE: Scholarly Resources.

———. 1989. *The Gallup Poll: Public Opinion 1988*. Wilmington, DE: Scholarly Resources.

———. 1993. *The Gallup Poll: Public Opinion 1992*. Wilmington, DE: Scholarly Resources.

———. 1997. *The Gallup Poll: Public Opinion 1996*. Wilmington, DE: Scholarly Resources.

Gallup News Service. 2000. "Poll Trends: Clinton Job Approval." Princeton, NJ: Gallup Organization. (Available at http://www.gallup.com/poll/trends/ptjobapp.asp.)

Gelman, Andrew and Gary King. 1993. "Why Are American Presidential Election Campaign Polls So Variable When Votes Are So Predictable?" *British Journal of Political Science* 23: 409–451.

Gleisner, Richard F. 1992. "Economic Determinants of Presidential Elections: The Fair Model." *Political Behavior* 14: 383–394.

Goodfellow, Kris. 1996. "Quick Calls: How America Gets the News." *New York Times* 6 November, A16.

Granger, C. W. J. 1989. *Forecasting in Business and Economics*. 2d. ed. San Diego, CA: Academic Press.

Greene, Jay P. 1993. "Forewarned Before Forecast: Presidential Election Forecasting Models and the 1992 Election." *PS: Political Science and Politics* 26: 17–21.

Haller, H. Brandon and Helmut Norpoth. 1994. "Let the Good Times Roll: The Economic Expectations of U.S. Voters." *American Journal of Political Science* 38: 625–650.

Haynes, Stephen E. and Joe A. Stone. 1994. "Why Did Economic Models Falsely Predict a Bush Landslide in 1992?" *Contemporary Economic Policy* 12: 123–130.

Hibbs, Douglas A., Jr. 1982. "President Reagan's Mandate from the 1980 Elections: A Shift to the Right?" *American Politics Quarterly* 10: 387–420.

———. 1987. *The American Political Economy: Macroeconomics and Electoral Politics*. Cambridge, MA: Harvard University Press.

Hirschman, Albert O. 1982. *Shifting Involvement: Private Interest and Public Action*. Princeton, NJ: Princeton University Press.

Holbrook, Thomas M. 1991. "Presidential Elections in Time and Space." *American Journal of Political Science* 35: 91–109.

———. 1996a. *Do Campaigns Matter?* Thousand Oaks, CA: Sage Publications.

———. 1996b. "Reading the Political Tea Leaves: A Forecasting Model of Contemporary Presidential Elections." *American Politics Quarterly* 24: 506–519; forecast addendum, 533.

———. 2000. "Reading the Political Tea Leaves: A Forecasting Model of Contemporary Presidential Elections." In *Before the Vote: Forecasting American National Elections*. eds. James E. Campbell and James C. Garand. Thousand Oaks, CA: Sage Publications. (Update of Holbrook 1996b.)

———. 2001a. "Forecasting with Mixed Economic Signals: A Cautionary Tale." *PS: Political Science and Politics* 34: 39–44.

———. 2001b. "(Mis)reading the Political Tea Leaves." *American Politics Research* 29: 297–301.

Institute for Social Research. University of Michigan. 1995. *American National Election Studies 1948–1994*. May. Compact Disk no. CD0010.

Irons, John S. 1996. "The Election Calculator." (Available at http://www.mit.edu/ people/ irons/myjava/ecalc.html.)

"It Could Be You." 2000. *Economist* 4 November, 31–32.

"It's Predictable: An Economist's [Ray Fair's] View of Presidential Elections." 1996. *New York Times* 2 January, C2.

Janis, Irving L. 1982. *Groupthink: Psychological Studies of Policy Decisions and Fiascoes.* 2d ed. Boston: Houghton Mifflin.

Kaiser, Robert G. 2000a. "Academics Say It's Elementary: Gore Wins." *Washington Post* 31 August, A12.

———. 2000b. "Is This Any Way to Pick a Winner?" *Washington Post* 26 May, A1.

Kelley, Stanley, Jr. 1983. *Interpreting Elections*. Princeton, NJ: Princeton University Press.

Kelley, Stanley, Jr. and Thad W. Mirer. 1974. "The Simple Act of Voting." *American Political Science Review* 68: 572–591.

Kenski, Henry C. and Edward C. Dreyer. 1977. "In Search of State Presidential Bellwethers." *Social Science Quarterly* 58: 498–505.

Kernell, Samuel. 2000. "Life Before Polls: Ohio Politicians Predict the 1828 Presidential Vote." *PS: Political Science and Politics* 33: 569–574.

Kinder, Donald R. and D. Roderick Kiewiet. 1981. "Sociotropic Politics: The American Case." *British Journal of Political Science* 11: 129–162.

Koretz, Gene. 1992. "Voters May Have a Jaundiced View of the Economy." *Business Week* 19 October, 22.

———. 1996. "It's Clinton—By a Landslide: So Says a Regional Economic Model." *Business Week* 4 November, 32.

———. 2000. "A Rising Tide Lifts . . . Al Gore: The Veep's Edge Is the Economy." *Business Week* 27 March, 30.

Lazarsfeld, Paul F., Bernard Berelson, and Hazel Gaudet. 1944. *The People's Choice: How the Voter Makes Up His Mind in a Presidential Campaign*. New York: Duell, Sloan and Pearce.

Lewis-Beck, Michael S. 1985. "Election Forecasts in 1984: How Accurate Were They?" *PS* 18: 53–62.

Lewis-Beck, Michael S. and Tom W. Rice. 1982. "Presidential Popularity and Presidential Vote." *Public Opinion Quarterly* 46: 534–537.

———. 1984. "Forecasting Presidential Elections: A Comparison of Naive Models." *Political Behavior* 6: 9–21.

———. 1992. *Forecasting Elections*. Washington: CQ Press.

Lewis-Beck, Michael S. and Charles Tien. 1996. "The Future in Forecasting: Prospective Presidential Models." *American Politics Quarterly* 24: 468–491; forecast addendum, 533.

———. 2000. "The Future in Forecasting: Prospective Presidential Models." In *Before the Vote: Forecasting American National Elections*. eds. James E. Campbell and James C. Garand. Thousand Oaks, CA: Sage Publications. (Update of Lewis-Beck and Tien 1996.)

———. 2001a. "Election 2000: How Wrong Was the Forecast?" *American Politics Research* 29: 302–306.

———. 2001b. "Modeling the Future: Lessons from the Gore Forecast." *PS: Political Science and Politics* 34: 21–23.

Lichtman, Allan J. 1996a. *The Keys to the White House, 1996: A Surefire Guide to Predicting the Next President*. Lanham, MD: Madison Books.

———. 1996b. "The Keys to the White House: Who Will Be the Next American President?" *Social Education* 60: 358–360.

————. 1996c. "Third-Party Presidential Candidates." Press briefing at USIA Foreign Press Center. 2 April. Washington, D.C. (Available at http://dns.usis-israel.org.il/publish/elections/fpc3pty.htm.)

————. 1999. "The Keys to Election 2000." *Social Education* 65: 422–424.

————. 2000. "The Keys to the White House 2000." *National Forum* 80: 13–16.

Lichtman, Allan J. and Ken DeCell. 1990. *The Thirteen Keys to the Presidency*. Lanham, MD: Madison Books.

Linstone, Harold A. and Murray Turoff. 1975. *The Delphi Method: Techniques and Applications*. Reading, MA: Addison-Wesley.

Lockerbie, Brad. 2000. "Election Forecasting: A Look to the Future." In *Before the Vote: Forecasting American National Elections*. eds. James E. Campbell and James C. Garand. Thousand Oaks, CA: Sage Publications.

————. 2001. "Forecast 2000: An Afterthought." *American Politics Research* 29: 307–312.

Lord, David. 1996. "Predict the Future Accurately Every Time: Who's Kidding Whom?" In *The Old Farmer's Almanac, 1997*. ed. Judson D. Hale, Sr. Dublin, NH: Yankee Publishing.

Makridakis, Spyros, Steven C. Wheelwright, and Rob J. Hyndman. 1998. *Forecasting: Methods and Applications*. 3d ed. New York: John Wiley and Sons.

Mann, Thomas. 2001. "Reflections on the 2000 U.S. Presidential Election." *Politique étrangère* January. (Available at http://www.brook.edu/views/articles/mann/2001politique.htm.)

"A Market for Votes." 2000. *Economist* 4 November, 84.

Markus, Gregory. 1988. "The Impact of Personal and National Economic Conditions on the Presidential Vote: A Pooled Cross-Sectional Analysis." *American Journal of Political Science* 32: 137–154.

Mason-Dixon Polling and Research, Inc. 2000. "Pennsylvania State Polls: Gore Holds Slim Lead in Pennsylvania." (Available at http://www.mason-dixon.com/stpolls.cfm?stpoll_id=132.)

Mayer, William G. 1996. "Forecasting Presidential Nominations." In *In Pursuit of the White House: How We Choose Our Presidential Nominees*. ed. William G. Mayer. Chatham, NJ: Chatham House Publishers.

McCullough, David. 1992. *Truman*. New York: Simon & Schuster.

Meier, Kenneth J. 1979. *Predicting Oklahoma Elections: An Inexpensive and Accurate Method with Oklahoma Election Statistics by County, 1970–1978*. Norman, OK: Bureau of Government Research, University of Oklahoma.

Miller, D. W. 2000. "Election Results Leave Political Scientists Defensive Over Forecasting Models." *Chronicle of Higher Education* 17 November, A24.

Miller, Warren E. and J. Merrill Shanks. 1996. *The New American Voter*. Cambridge, MA: Harvard University Press.

Miller, Warren E. and Santa Traugott. 1989. *American National Election Studies Data Sourcebook, 1952–1986*. Cambridge, MA: Harvard University Press.

Mitofsky, Warren J. 1991. "A Short History of Exit Polls." In *Polling and Presidential Election Coverage*. eds. Paul J. Lavrakas and Jack K. Holley. Newbury Park, CA: Sage Publications.

Norpoth, Helmut. 1995. "Is Clinton Doomed? An Early Forecast for 1996." *PS: Political Science and Politics* 28: 201–207.

————. 1996. "Of Time and Candidates: A Forecast for 1996." *American Politics Quarterly* 24: 443–467; forecast addendum, 534.

————. 2000a. "Of Time and Candidates: A Forecast for 1996." In *Before the Vote: Forecasting American National Elections*. eds. James E. Campbell and James C. Garand. Thousand Oaks, CA: Sage Publications. (Update of Norpoth 1996.)

———. 2000b. "Primary Colors: A Forecast of the 2000 Presidential Election." Paper presented at the annual meeting of the American Political Science Association. Washington, D.C.

———. 2001a. "'Of Time and Candidates' Revised: Too Generous for Al Gore." *American Politics Research* 29: 313–319.

———. 2001b. "Primary Colors: A Mixed Blessing for Al Gore." *PS: Political Science and Politics* 34: 45–48.

Organski, A. F. K. 1997. Personal communication to the author, 30 August.

Organski, A. F. K. and Bruce Bueno de Mesquita. 1993. "Forecasting the 1992 French Referendum." In *New Diplomacy in the Post-Cold War World: Essays for Susan Strange*. eds. Roger Morgan et al. New York: St. Martin's Press.

Ornstein, Norman. 1995. "Who Will Win the White House?" *Fortune* 30 October, 51–52.

Palmer, Kenneth T., G. Thomas Taylor, and Marcus A. LiBrizzi. 1992. *Maine Politics and Government*. Lincoln, NE: University of Nebraska Press.

Passell, Peter. 1996. "Sideshows Aside, Economy Is Still Key to Election." *New York Times* 2 January, C2.

Pennar, Karen. 1992. "The Economists' Ouija Boards Spell 'George'." *Business Week* 3 August, 16.

Petersen, Svend. 1968. *A Statistical History of the American Presidential Elections*. New York: Frederick Ungar Publishing Co.

Pindyck, Robert S. and Daniel L. Rubinfeld. 1998. *Econometric Models and Economic Forecasts*. 4th ed. New York: Irwin McGraw-Hill.

Pool, Ithiel de Sola, Robert P. Abelson, and Samuel L. Popkin. 1965. *Candidates, Issues, and Strategies: A Computer Simulation of the 1960 and 1964 Presidential Elections*. rev. ed. Cambridge, MA: MIT Press.

Ray, James Lee and Bruce Russett. 1996. "The Future As Arbiter of Theoretical Controversies: Predictions, Explanations and the End of the Cold War." *British Journal of Political Science* 26: 441–470.

Renshaw, Edward and Emery Trahan. 1990. "Presidential Elections and the Federal Reserve's Interest Rate Reaction Function." *Journal of Policy Modeling* 12: 29–34.

Reston, James. 1992. *Deadline: A Memoir*. New York: Times Books.

Rice, Tom W. 1985. "Predicting Presidential Elections: A Review Essay." *Western Political Quarterly* 38: 675–686.

Robinson, Claude E. 1932. *Straw Votes: A Study of Political Prediction*. New York: Columbia University Press.

Roemer, John E. 1995. "Political Cycles." *Economics and Politics* 7: 1–20.

Rosenof, Theodore. 1999. "The Legend of Louis Bean: Political Prophecy and the 1948 Election." *Historian* 62: 63–78.

Rosenstone, Steven J. 1983. *Forecasting Presidential Elections*. New Haven, CT: Yale University Press.

Rowe, Gene and George Wright. 1999. "The Delphi Technique As a Forecasting Tool: Issues and Analysis." *International Journal of Forecasting* 15: 353–375.

Rowe, Gene, George Wright, and Fergus Bolger. 1991. "The Delphi Technique: a Reevaluation of Research and Theory." *Technological Forecasting and Social Change* 39: 235–251.

Runyon, John H., Jennefer Verdini, and Sally S. Runyon. 1971. *Source Book of American Presidential Campaign and Election Statistics, 1948–1968*. New York: Frederick Ungar.

Scammon, Richard M., Alice V. McGillivray. comp. and eds. 1995. *America Votes 21: A Handbook of Contemporary American Election Statistics*. 1994 ed. Washington: Elections Research Center and Congressional Quarterly.

Scammon, Richard M., Alice V. McGillivray, and Rhodes Cook. 1997. *America Votes 22: A Handbook of Contemporary American Election Statistics*. 1996 ed. Washington: Congressional Quarterly.

Schlesinger, Arthur M., Jr. 1986. *The Cycles of American History*. Boston: Houghton Mifflin.

Schlesinger, Arthur M. (Sr.) 1949. *Paths to the Present*. New York: Macmillan.

Shaw, Daron R. 1999a. "The Effect of TV Ads and Candidate Appearances on Statewide Presidential Votes." *American Political Science Review* 93: 345–361.

———. 1999b. "A Study of Presidential Campaign Effects from 1952 to 1992." *Journal of Politics* 61: 387–422.

Shea, Christopher. 1996. "A Small Branch of Political Science Seeks to Perfect the Art of Election Forecasting." *Chronicle of Higher Education* 25 October, A18.

Sigelman, Lee. 1979. "Presidential Popularity and Presidential Elections." *Public Opinion Quarterly* 43: 532–534.

Simon, Herbert A. 1954. "Bandwagon and Underdog Effects of Election Predictions." *Public Opinion Quarterly* 18: 245–253.

Spiers, Joseph. 1992. "A Model for Bush–Plug in the Numbers and He Wins." *Fortune* 7 September, 22.

Squire, Peverill. 1988. "Why the 1936 Literary Digest Poll Failed." *Public Opinion Quarterly* 52: 125–133.

Stimson, James A. 1991. *Public Opinion in America: Moods, Cycles, and Swings*. Boulder, CO: Westview Press.

Stoken, Dick A. 1990. *Strategic Investment Timing in the 90's: How to Pinpoint and Profit from Short and Long-Term Changes in the Economy*. rev. ed. Chicago: Probus Publishing Co.

Survey Research Center. Institute for Social Research. University of Michigan. 2001. "Survey of Consumers." Tables 4, 6, and 15. (Available at http://athena.sca.isr. umich.edu.)

Tankard, James W., Jr. 1992. "Public Opinion Polling by Newspapers in the Presidential Election Campaign of 1824." *Journalism Quarterly* 49: 361–365.

Tetlock, Philip E. and Aaron Belkin, eds. 1996a. *Counterfactual Thought Experiments in World Politics*. Princeton, NJ: Princeton University Press.

———. 1996b. "Historical Counterfactuals and Conditional Forecasts in World Politics: Potential Biases and Possible Correctives." Paper presented at the annual meeting of the American Political Science Association. San Francisco.

Traugott, Michael W. and Vincent Price. 1992. "Exit Polls in the 1989 Virginia Gubernatorial Race: Where Did They Go Wrong?" *Public Opinion Quarterly* 56: 245–253.

Tufte, Edward R. 1974. *Data Analysis for Politics and Policy*. Englewood Cliffs, NJ: Prentice-Hall.

———. 1978. *Political Control of the Economy*. Princeton, NJ: Princeton University Press.

Tufte, Edward R. and Richard A. Sun. 1975. "Are There Bellwether Electoral Districts?" *Public Opinion Quarterly* 39: 1–18.

U.S. Bureau of Economic Analysis. 1996a. "Historical Data for Selected Series: Yield on New Series of High-Grade Corporate Bonds." *Survey of Current Business* January/February, Table 116.

———. 1996b. "Historical Data for Selected Series: Composite Index of 11 Leading Indicators, Change Over 3-Month Span." *Survey of Current Business* March, Table 910c.

———. 1998. "GDP and Other Major NIPA Series, 1929–97." *Survey of Current Business*. August. Table 2A. (Available at http://www.bea.doc.gov/bea/dn/0898nip3.pdf.)

———. 2001. "NIPA Tables." (Available at http://www.bea.gov/bea/dn/nipaweb.)

U.S. Bureau of the Census. 1975. *Historical Statistics of the United States, Colonial Times to 1970*. pt 2. Washington: Government Printing Office.

―――. 1996. *Statistical Abstract of the United States: 1996*. Washington: Government Printing Office.

―――. 2000. *Statistical Abstract of the United States: 2000*. Washington: Government Printing Office.

U.S. Federal Election Commission. 2001. "2000 Official Presidential General Election Results." 18 January. (Available at http://fecweb1.fec.gov/pubrec/2000 presgeresults. htm.)

U.S. Federal Reserve. 2000. "Average Yield to Maturity on Selected Long-Term Bonds, Average of Daily Data." (Available at http:\\www.federalreserve.gov/releases/H15/data/wf/aaa.txt.)

U.S. House of Representatives. 1985. *Uniform Poll Closing: Hearings Held Before the Subcommittee on Elections of the Committee on House Administration*. May, July, August. Washington: Government Printing Office.

Visser, Penny S., Jon A. Krosnick, Jesse Marquette, and Michael Curtin. 1996. "Mailing Surveys for Election Forecasting? An Evaluation of the *Columbus Dispatch* Poll." *Public Opinion Quarterly* 60: 181–227.

White, E. B. 1990. *Writings from the New Yorker, 1927–1976*. ed. Rebecca M. Dale. New York: HarperPerennial.

Wlezien, Christopher. 2001. "On Forecasting the Presidential Vote." *PS: Political Science and Politics* 34: 25–31.

Wlezien, Christopher and Robert S. Erikson. 1996. "Temporal Horizons and Presidential Election Forecasts." *American Politics Quarterly* 24: 492–505; forecast addendum, 534.

―――. 2000. "Temporal Horizons and Presidential Election Forecasts." In *Before the Vote: Forecasting American National Elections*. eds. James E. Campbell and James C. Garand. Thousand Oaks, CA: Sage Publications. (Update of Wlezien and Erikson 1996.)

―――. 2001. "After the Election: Our Forecast in Retrospect." *American Politics Research* 29: 320–328.

Wright, George and Peter Ayton. eds. 1987. *Judgmental Forecasting*. New York: John Wiley and Sons.

Appendix:
A Brief Introduction
to Regression

This appendix provides an elementary explanation of the statistical technique of regression and demonstrates how regression can be used to produce forecasts of the vote in presidential elections. The easiest way to understand regression is to visualize it graphically, which is the approach taken here.

At the outset, we must identify the phenomenon being studied, what is sometimes termed the "unit of analysis." In this example, the object of study is presidential election years, specifically the 11 years (at 4-year intervals) from 1952 through 1992 in which presidential elections were held. I have chosen two characteristics of each of these years to analyze, the vote in the presidential election and the health of the national economy. Numerical indicators reflecting these characteristics are also selected. In this case, the vote characteristic is represented by the percentage of the vote received by the presidential candidate of the incumbent president's party. (More specifically, this is the percentage of the "two-party" vote, the combined vote for the Democratic and Republican candidates, omitting votes received by other candidates.) The indicator representing the state of the economy is the percent change in real gross domestic product (GDP) during the first half of the election year.

Regression is a means by which to compare the 11 election years on the basis of these two indicators and to test the notion that one may influence the other. The initial objective is to identify patterns in which the two indicators—variables—vary together. For example, in election years in which the value of one characteristic (GDP growth rate) increases, does the value of the other characteristic (vote for the candidate of the incumbent party) also increase? And in other election years in which GDP growth is low, is that also true of the incumbent party vote? If so, we would conclude that the two characteristics are related—that a co-relationship or "correlation" exists between them. This example, in which both indicators vary in the same direction reflects a positive correlation between them. (It is also possible that they consistently vary in opposite directions, in which case a negative correlation would exist.)

When two variables consistently vary together—have strong correlations—it may be that one is influencing the other, causing its variation. This is by no means necessarily true, but it is a cue for the analyst familiar with the subject to investigate the relationship further. A variable that is thought to be caused by another is called the "dependent" variable because its values depend on values of the other variable, the "independent" variable. The independent variable is considered to be the source of variation in the dependent variable and, in fact, the likely *cause* of that variation. In this case, the independent variable is growth rate in GDP, and the dependent variable is the incumbent party candidate's share of the two-party vote. Thus, the presumption is that variation in economic growth may be influencing—causing—variation in the vote.

Only when it makes sense to conclude theoretically that GDP *could* influence the vote should we undertake regression analysis. Can a reasonable case be made that the state of the economy influences election outcomes? Yes. The gist of the argument, stated in Chapter 8, is this: "When the economy is doing well, people are happy with the status quo and might vote to keep the same party in the White House. When the economy is performing poorly, people could well want a change, hoping that a new president's policies would improve the economy." Once we are satisfied that there are sound reasons why the independent variable could influence dependent variable, we can proceed on to regression to determine whether this supposition can be verified.

We begin a visual explanation of regression by graphing data on the vote and on economic growth for each election. This is done by creating a "scatterplot." First the sides (or "axes") of the plot are drawn, as shown in each of the accompanying figures. The axis for the variable being predicted—the dependent variable—is on the left side and positioned vertically. The symbol for that indicator is "Y." The variable that presumably influences the vote, the "independent" variable, is scaled horizontally on the bottom side; its symbol is "X."

Once the sides of the scatterplot are formed, we are ready to plot the data points. A data point is the place on the scatterplot where, for a particular election, the value for the vote and the value for GDP growth intersect. Thus, for example, in 1952 the GDP growth rate in the first half was 1 percent. In the 1952 election, the percentage of the two-party vote for the incumbent party candidate—Democrat Stevenson—was 45 percent. (In the interest of simplicity, all data in this explanation of two-variable regression are rounded off to the nearest whole number.) The values for these two variables intersect at the point marked "1952" in Figure A.1.

In similar fashion, data points for all 11 presidential elections from 1952 through 1992 are entered on the scatterplot, with the result depicted in Figure A.2.

The next step is to plot a line, running from side to side, in the center of the group of election points. The goal is to place the line as close as possible to all of the elections. By observing where elections fall on the plot, we can visualize approximately where the line should be drawn for it to be in the middle of the points. The regression technique, however, tells us *exactly* where to put the line, so that it is placed absolutely as close as possible to the group of points. In fact, it is mathematically impossible for the combined squared vertical distances between the points and the line to be any less. (See Figure A.3) This line—known as the regression line—represents the composite of the group of elections.

To determine where the regression line is placed on the plot, first imagine a line rising vertically from the zero point on the horizontal axis, that is, from the point of zero change in GDP. In Figure A.4, this is represented by a vertical dashed line. As seen in the figure, the regression line intersects this zero GDP vertical line at a point called the "intercept" or "constant." In this example, the intercept is 49 percent on the vote (Y) axis.

We now need to know precisely how to angle the line from the intercept through the election points. The "regression coefficient" or "slope" is important for this purpose. The slope is the amount of change in the dependent variable (Y) that is produced by one unit of increase in the independent variable (X). In this case, the slope is the amount of increase in the vote percentage received by the incumbent party candidate that is produced by 1 percent increase in GDP. As shown in Figure A.4, to plot the regression line

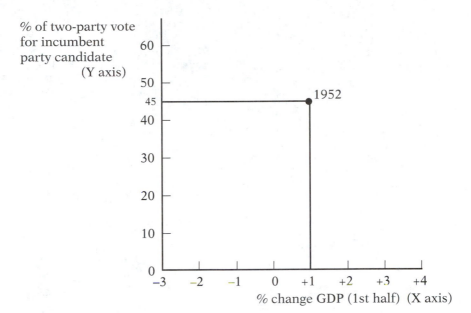

Figure A.1

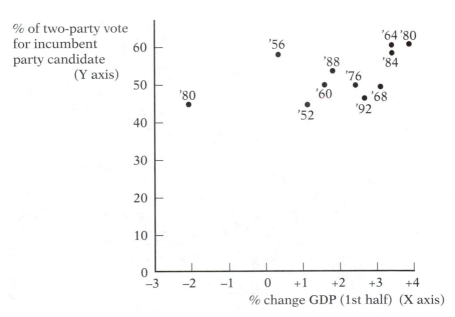

Figure A.2

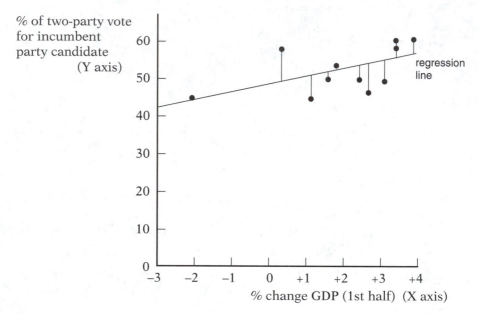

Figure A.3

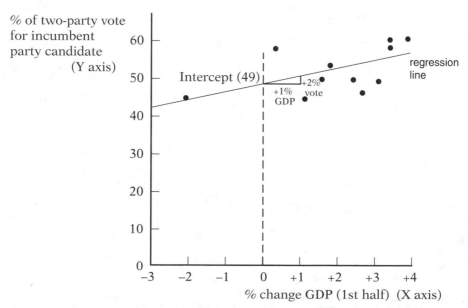

Figure A.4

we start at the intercept, on the vertical line above zero GDP at 49 percent on the vote scale. From the intercept we count to the right one unit on the horizontal X scale, which is 1 percent increase in GDP growth. From that point, we then count up vertically a distance equal to the value of the slope, which is 2 percent on the vote scale. If we draw a line between the intercept and this point—and extend it in both directions across the plot—that is precisely where the regression line should be.

A useful measure of the closeness of the line to the election points is r^2, the "coefficient of determination." Values for this measure vary between zero and one. When r^2 is near one, this means that the election points, as a group, are very close to the regression line; the distances between the points and the line, depicted in Figure A.3, are short. In that case, the regression line would quite accurately represent the composite of the election points. Stated another way, there is little "error" in the regression when the total distances between the election points and the line are short; the regression has accounted for variation in the elections well. At the other extreme, when r^2 is low, the data points are far from the line, and in fact they may not have much of a pattern at all. In this situation, it is of little use to place a regression line through the center of the election points because the line would not represent them well. The error in the regression would be high.

To make an election forecast in which we can have confidence, the election points should be arrayed in a distinct, tight pattern around the regression line, which would result in a high r^2 value. If these assumptions for the historical data are met, an approximate forecast can be produced merely by plotting a recent value for the independent variable on the line and then noting where that point is on the dependent variable scale. For example, suppose that in late July 1996 we were attempting to forecast the outcome of the 1996 presidential election. By that time we would have known that GDP grew in the first half by 3 percent. Accordingly, we note the 3 percent point on the horizontal GDP axis at the bottom of the plot, and then draw a straight perpendicular line up to the regression line, as depicted in Figure A.5. From that point on the regression

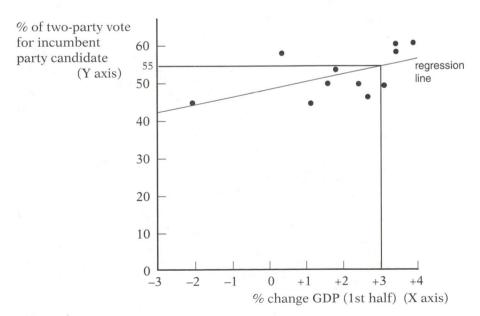

Figure A.5

line, we draw a horizontal line left to the vote axis. The value on the vote axis at that point is the forecast of the vote, which appears to be about 55 percent.

There is a more precise way to calculate this forecast, using a regression equation, which has this basic form:

estimate of
of dependent = intercept + slope *times* value for
variable (Y) independent variable (X)

As applied to this forecasting example, the equation would be:

forecast = intercept + (slope *times* value for GDP)
of vote

In this case, the intercept is 49, the slope is 2, and the first half GDP growth rate is 3. The equation, therefore, becomes:

forecast
of '96 vote = 49 + (2 × 3)
= 49 + 6
= 55

This calculation is depicted visually in Figure A.6. Beginning at zero on the GDP scale, we count up to the intercept, which is 49 on the vote scale. From that point, we begin the process of adding the amount of increase in the vote for the 3 percent increase in GDP. In the figure, this is represented as a three-step process because we are modeling the effects of a 3 percent increase in GDP, 1 percent at a time. Each 1 percent rise in GDP results in an additional 2 percent in the vote for the incumbent party candidate. Thus, beginning with the 49 percent intercept, we add 2 percent to the vote for the *first* percent increase in GDP. Moving up in stair-step manner, we add another

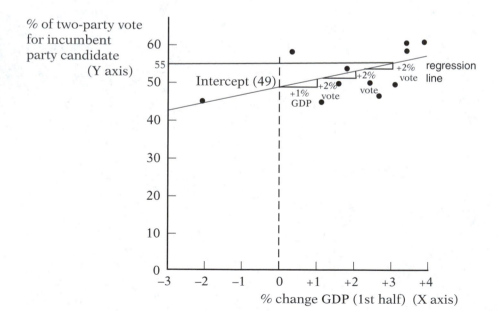

Figure A.6

2 percent for the *second* percent increase in GDP, plus still another 2 percent for the *third* percent increase in GDP. This adds up to 55 percent (49% + 2% + 2% + 2%), which is the forecast of the vote when GDP has increased 3 percent. In essence, it is this process that the regression equation computes when it is used to produce forecasts.

More than one independent (causal) variable can be used in regression, but it is difficult to illustrate graphically. The multiple-variable equation is set up in this manner:

forecast
of vote = intercept + (slope [for var 1] *times* value for variable **1**)
+ (slope [for var 2] *times* value for variable **2**)
+ (slope [for var 3] *times* value for variable **3**)

Suppose that we calculate an equation with two independent variables: first half GDP and June presidential approval ratings. The regression equation would take this form:

forecast
of vote = intercept + (slope [for GDP] *times* **GDP**)
for '96
+ (slope [for pres. app.] *times* **pres. approval rating**)

Computations by computer indicate that the slope for GDP growth is 1.2, and the slope for presidential approval ratings is 0.3. (Note that the slope for GDP has changed somewhat in the presence of a second independent variable, which is typical.)

Using calculations to one decimal point, in 1996 GDP growth rate for the first half of the year was 2.7 percent and the presidential approval rating for June was 58 percent. Entering these values into the equation, the forecast for the 1996 presidential election outcome would have been computed in this manner:

forecast
of '96 vote = 34 + (1.2 × 2.7) + (.3 × 58)
= 34 + 3.2 + 17.4
= 54.6

(Incidentally, President Clinton's share of the two-party vote in 1996 was 54.7 percent.)

There is, of course, more to regression than has been presented here. But, as is evident, the essence of the concept is quite simple and straightforward. It is a technique well suited to making forecasts from patterns evident in historical data.

Glossary:
Common Terms Used
In Regression

Descriptions of the following terms are tailored to the subject of this book and assume that the cases are election years and that the dependent variable is election outcomes.

adjusted r^2 (R^2). See **coefficient of determination.**

autocorrelation. Autocorrelation is a problem that exists in regression when the errors in fitting the independent variables to the elections in the historical data set are correlated with the errors of preceding elections. (See **error.**) The most common problem of this type is *first order* autocorrelation, which occurs when election errors are correlated with the errors of the immediately preceding election. Thus, suppose that we set up two columns of numbers in which on the first row the error for the 1996 election is in the first column and the error for the 1992 election is in the second column; on the second row the error for the 1992 election is similarly paired with the error for the 1988 election; and so on through the series of elections. If these two columns of errors are significantly correlated, then first order autocorrelation exists. The problem of first order autocorrelation can be detected by the Durbin-Watson test. (See **Durbin-Watson test.**)

autoregressive models; autoregression. Autoregressive models are regressions in which previous values of the dependent variable (election results) are used as independent variables. The length of these time lags can vary. Results from the immediate prior election could be used as an independent variable; results from two elections prior also could be used, as could other lagged intervals. In autoregressive models the obvious assumption is that past election results have an impact on later elections. (See **lag.**)

coefficient of determination (r^2, R^2, adjusted R^2). The coefficient of determination for a regression is a measure of the proportion of variation in election outcomes (the variance) that is explained by the independent variable(s). The degree of success of the independent variable in explaining the election results is represented by the regression line. Thus, the coefficient of determination can be thought of as the squared correlation between the regression's estimates of the election results (which are points on the regression line) and the actual election results. The coefficient of determination is denoted by the letter r^2 when there is one independent variable, and by R^2 when there are two or more. Either R^2 or r^2 can be converted to a percentage by multiplying by 100. Thus a R^2 of .80 means that the independent variables account for 80 percent of the variation in election outcomes. The square root of r^2 or R^2 is the correlation coefficient. (See **correlation coefficient.**)

An alternate measure of R^2 is the adjusted R^2, which takes into account the number of elections in the data set and the number of independent variables. It is appropriate to use the adjusted R^2 when there is a small number of cases (elections), as is common in this book. For most of the equations that I have presented, both R^2 and adjusted R^2 are reported.

confidence interval. The forecast confidence interval (or margin of error) indicates the range of election outcomes within which a predicted election result can be expected to occur, with a given probability. Suppose that a candidate is predicted to receive 55 percent of the vote with a 95 percent confidence interval of $+/-4$ percent. This means that there is a 95 percent probability that the actual vote for that candidate will be between 51 percent and 59 percent. In essence, the width of the confidence interval depends on two factors: how well the regression fits the set of past elections and the number of elections in the data set.

constant. In a regression, the constant or intercept is the point in a scatterplot at which the regression line crosses the vertical Y axis (which represents election outcomes) when the value for the independent variable is zero. (See the Appendix for a more detailed description.)

correlation; correlation coefficient (r). The correlation coefficient, denoted by the symbol r is a measure of association between two variables. For example, when we say that the GDP growth rate is highly correlated with election results, this means that a high value for r exists between these two variables. Significance tests are usually performed when r is calculated. These indicate the extent to which there is a possibility that the correlation between two variables is due merely to chance. When the possibility of a chance relationship is sufficiently low, usually 5 percent or less, we can say that the two variables are "significantly correlated." The correlation coefficient squared (r^2) becomes the coefficient of determination. (See **coefficient of determination.**)

dependent variable. The dependent variable in a regression is an indicator representing the phenomenon to be explained and predicted. In this book, the dependent variable is an indicator of the outcome of presidential elections.

dummy variable. A dummy variable, used in regression, is a column of zeros and ones. This type of variable is used to include dichotomies in the equation, such as the party affiliation of the president, which might be coded: 1 = Republican; 0 = Democrat (or vice versa).

Durbin-Watson test. The Durbin-Watson test reveals the extent to which first order autocorrelation is a problem in regression. (See **autocorrelation.**) Durbin-Watson values range between 0 and 4, with a score of 2.0 being optimal. Tables in appendices of most statistics books show the user how far above or below 2.0 a Durbin-Watson value can be before autocorrelation is a problem. For example, for a regression that includes 11 elections and two independent variables in the data set, a Durbin-Watson value between 1.604 and 2.396 would indicate the absence of first order autocorrelation with a 95 percent probability.

error. Error can be used in two ways. *First*, error can refer to the extent to which the regression line misses the election data points in the data set from which the regression was calculated. The distance between an election point and the line is the error for that election. This error is also referred to as the residual—that is, the "residue" that the regression cannot explain. The standard error of the estimate is a summary measure of all of the errors for the individual data points. (See **standard error of the estimate.**) *Second*, error also can refer to the extent that a forecast differs from the actual result. In this context forecast error is the difference between a predicted election result and the actual outcome of the election.

ex ante forecast. An ex ante forecast is a prediction of the future for which the analyst does not know the outcome. That is, at the time of the forecast the predicted event has yet to occur, and its outcome is thus unknown. A forecast made in July of the November general election result is an ex ante forecast.

ex post forecast. An ex post forecast is a "prediction" of a past event for which the outcome is known. Ex post forecasts often are used to test prediction models. For example, an analyst in 2001, using a regression model based on election data from 1952 through 1992, predicts the 1996 election outcome. Such ex post forecasts are numerous in this book.

F statistic. In multiple regression, the F statistic provides a test as to whether the regression *as a whole* is significant. This can be interpreted as a significance test of R^2. In testing the significance of the entire equation, the F test complements the t test, which tests the significance of individual independent variables in the regression.

independent variable. An independent variable in a regression is an indicator that is assumed to influence or cause the dependent variable (election outcomes), and thus may be used to predict future values of it. In a simple regression, there is only one independent variable in the equation. In a multiple regression, there are two or more independent variables.

intercept. See **constant.**

lag; lagged variable. In regression, a lagged variable is an independent variable whose values are from an earlier period than the dependent variable. For example, if in an equation interest rates a year before an election affect the election results, the interest rate variable has a one-year lagged effect. Autoregressive models use previous periods of the dependent variable as independent variables. (See **autoregressive models.**) "Distributed" lag regression equations use two or more previous time periods of an independent variable as separate additional independent variables.

lead; leading indicator. Lead is the interval between one point in time and some event in the future that is being predicted. For example, suppose that we are interested in determining the lead time of public opinion polls, measuring the public's support for candidates, in accurately predicting results of an upcoming election. If results of the polls made in early September accurately predict the early November election outcome, we could say that the polls lead the election by two months. They thus would be an effective leading indicator.

margin of error. See **confidence interval.**

model. In the context of this study, a model is a regression equation that purports to explain past election outcomes using several independent (causal) variables. The patterns evident in the historical data, as identified in the regression, can be used to predict future election results from later values of the independent variables.

multicollinearity. Multicollinearity is a problem that occurs in multiple regression when some or all of the independent variables are highly correlated with one another. If multicollinearity is present, election forecasts produced by the regression are unreliable. A common test for multicollinearity is to calculate regressions in which each independent variable is, in turn, treated as a dependent variable and regressed on the remaining independent variables. If the R^2 for one of these equations is high and the F test is significant, multicollinearity is likely present.

multiple regression. Multiple regression is a form of regression in which two or more independent variables are assumed to influence or cause the dependent variable (election outcomes). When used for prediction, forecasts are generated by the multiple independent variables. (See the Appendix.)

multivariate. This term refers to two or more variables. In particular, a multivariate equation is one which has two or more independent (causal) variables. To reduce the use of jargon in this book the term "multi-variable" is used in lieu of "multivariate," except in chapter 9.

N. The letter N refers to the number of cases used in a regression model. In this study, the cases are election years, so N refers to the number of election years in a regression.

r^2, R^2. See **coefficient of determination.**

regression. See **multiple regression, simple regression,** and the Appendix.

regression coefficient. See **slope.**

residual. See **error.**

significance. Significance is a measure of the possibility that a statistical relationship found to exist between variables is due merely to chance. For example, in Table 1.1, we found that the relationship between June trial heats and election results was significant at the .017 level when using a t-test. Multiplying the significance value by 100 reveals that there is only a 1.7 percent possibility that the relationship between these two variables is due merely to chance. Subtracting that value from 100 percent, we can say that a 98.3 percent probability exists that the relationship is *not* due to chance. Normally, we want significance probabilities greater than 95 percent, that is, significance levels at the .05 level or less.

simple regression. Simple regression is a form of regression analysis in which only one independent variable is assumed to influence or cause the dependent variable. In a forecasting application, predictions would be generated from the one independent variable. (See the Appendix.)

slope; regression coefficient. In a regression, the slope or regression coefficient is a measure of the amount of change in the election results for one unit of change in an independent variable. (See the Appendix for a more detailed explanation.)

standard deviation. See **variance**.

standard error of the estimate. The standard error of the estimate is a measure of the extent to which a regression line fits the data points in a scatterplot. It denotes variation of the data points around the line and is adjusted for the number of cases (elections) in the data set. An important use of the standard error of the estimate is in determining the confidence interval for forecasts. When used for this purpose, the standard error of the estimate is adjusted for certain characteristics of the independent variable and multiplied by the t value for the confidence interval desired (e.g., 95%).

t-test. The t-test is used in regression to determine the significance of individual independent variables, doing so by determining the significance of the variable's slope (regression coefficient). Significance probabilities are derived from the t-test values. (See **significance.**)

variance; standard deviation. The variance of a column of data is a composite measure of the distance between each score in the column and the mean (average) of all of those scores, which is adjusted for the number of scores. When the value of the variance is low, the scores are mostly close to the mean; when the variance is high, they are far from the mean. In this book, the objective of regression is to account for this variation of scores around the mean in the dependent variable, the election outcomes. The standard deviation is merely the square root of the variance.

Index